THE DATA LOOM

THE DATA LOOM

Weaving Understanding by Thinking Critically and Scientifically with Data

STEPHEN FEW

Analytics Press

Analytics Press

PO Box 4933
El Dorado Hills, CA 95762
SAN 253-5602
www.analyticspress.com
Email: info@analyticspress.com

PUBLISHER: Bryan Pierce

COPY EDITOR: Nan Wishner
COMPOSITION: Bryan Pierce
COVER DESIGN: Nigel Holmes
PHOTOGRAPHY: Leanne Kruse
PRINTER AND BINDER: C&C Offset Printing Company

ISBN: 978-1-938377-11-2

This book was printed on acid-free paper in China.

10 9 8 7 6 5 4 3 2 1

ABOUT THE AUTHOR

Stephen Few, a longtime information professional, is best known for his contributions to the field of data visualization. Since founding his consultancy *Perceptual Edge* in 2003, he has written six books:

Show Me the Numbers: Designing Tables and Graphs to Enlighten (2nd edition)

Information Dashboard Design: Displaying Data for At-A-Glance Monitoring (2nd edition)

Now You See It: Simple Visualization Techniques for Quantitative Analysis

Signal: Understanding What Matters in a World of Noise

Big Data, Big Dupe: A Little Book About a Big Bunch of Nonsense

The Data Loom: Weaving Understanding by Thinking Critically and Scientifically with Data

Above all else, Stephen is a teacher. He believes that deriving value from data to support better decisions and actions is highly skilled work. Helping people develop these skills is his passion.

Stephen currently resides near Portland, Oregon with his two dogs, Enzo and Bella.

TABLE OF CONTENTS

CHAPTER 1 – CONSTRUCT A LOOM   1

Data sensemaking—the ability to weave data into understanding—requires a spectrum of skills. Critical thinking and scientific thinking are foremost among them.

CHAPTER 2 – THINK CRITICALLY   13

When we think critically, we apply logic and avoid cognitive biases.

CHAPTER 3 – THINK SCIENTIFICALLY   47

When we think scientifically, we apply the scientific method.

CHAPTER 4 – QUESTION THE DATA   67

Thinking critically and scientifically leads us to ask essential questions about data to improve the reliability of our findings.

CHAPTER 5 – MEASURE WISELY   83

Metrics can be powerful, but we often measure the wrong things, measure the right things ineffectively, and use measurements in harmful ways.

CHAPTER 6 – DEVELOP GOOD THINKING HABITS   103

In addition to critical thinking and scientific thinking, data sensemaking is also enriched by developing good thinking habits.

CHAPTER 7 – DEVELOP A DATA-SENSEMAKING CULTURE   111

Effective data sensemaking is undermined by most organizational cultures. We must promote the cultural changes that are needed to embrace critical and scientific thinking with data.

EPILOGUE – EMBRACE THE OPPORTUNITY   121

CHAPTER 1 – CONSTRUCT A LOOM

Data has been fetishized in recent years, but data, in and of itself, does not deserve our adulation. If "data is the new oil," just as oil is only useful once it's refined, data is only useful once we process it into understanding. Acquiring data is of no use if we don't have and apply the skills needed to understand it. Furthermore, misunderstanding data can lead to harm. And even once data is understood, it is of little value unless we use what we learn from it to make good decisions and then act on them. The better we understand the world, the better we'll survive and flourish in it. Great potential exists in data, but it can only be realized if great potential exists in us. To reach our potential, we must develop the right skills.

Most of the data that's being produced today is noise, and most of that will forever remain noise. To derive value from data, we must find and separate the signals from the noise. Back in 1939, the poet Edna St. Vincent Millay wrote these prescient words:

> Upon this gifted age, in its dark hour,
> rains from the sky a meteoric shower
> of facts...they lie, unquestioned, uncombined.
> Wisdom enough to leach us of our ill
> is daily spun, but there exists no loom
> to weave it into a fabric.[1]

Even though she wrote these words long before the so-called information age, Millay accurately described our situation today. We live in a time when facts abound, but our ability to weave those facts into a meaningful and useful fabric is lagging far behind their availability. Sadly, most people who work with data have not discovered the loom that's needed to weave facts into understanding.

I've worked as an information professional for more than 35 years. During most of the last 15 of those years, my work focused on data visualization. This changed recently when I broadened the scope to consider the full set of skills that we need to derive understanding, and thus value, from data. Data visualization provides powerful techniques for exploring, making sense of, and communicating data, especially when we need to understand quantitative patterns and relationships, but it's of little value unless data visualization techniques are complemented by other essential skills. No matter how well we visualize data, it's meaningless and useless if we mishandle the data in other ways. Misunderstood data, powerfully visualized, is worse than worthless; it can be downright dangerous.

A Spectrum of Thinking Skills

To understand quantitative data, we must move past just counting things to thinking deeply about them. This thinking involves several skill sets that work in concert:

- *Domain knowledge*
  To understand data in a particular domain, we must understand that domain to a fair degree. The greater our knowledge of a domain, the better equipped we are in most situations to make sense of its data. For example, to understand sales data, we must have a basic understanding of sales in our organization, including the objectives and processes. This is true for every domain (medicine, education, finance, etc.). As Randall K. Noon wrote:

  > *Applying a method is not a substitute for basic subject matter knowledge, evidence, or facts. If there were a heart transplant failure case that needed to be investigated, I don't think a group of bricklayers would do as good a job in figuring out the issues as would a group of doctors and surgeons. Conversely, in a controversy involving masonry workmanship, I believe that a group of bricklayers would*

do a better job than a team of doctors and surgeons.
Methodology is simply a framework within which subject
matter knowledge, evidence, and facts are organized and
assessed.[2]

Data analysis is riddled with examples of misunderstandings
that resulted from a lack of domain knowledge, regardless of
how talented and skilled the analysts were. When we apply
general skills to a specific domain, we need knowledge of that
domain to shape and apply those skills.

- *Critical thinking skills*
  We must know how to investigate and validate or disprove our
  assumptions, overcome cognitive biases, reason logically, ask
  the right questions, and prioritize work based on our
  objectives.
- *Scientific thinking skills*
  We must understand the scientific method and know how to
  apply it, especially the ability to formulate and test
  hypotheses.
- *Statistical thinking skills*
  We must understand and know how to apply the basic
  principles and practices of statistics (i.e., quantitative
  reasoning).
- *Systems thinking skills*
  We must understand how things interact, often in complex
  ways, to form systems, including the ways in which the
  actions and interactions of parts affect the whole.
- *Visual thinking skills*
  We must know how to use visual representations to see and
  understand patterns and relationships in quantitative data.
- *Ethical thinking skills*
  We must understand how our findings will be used and the
  potential benefits, costs, and harms of those uses.

Making sense of quantitative data involves a seamless collaboration
of these somewhat distinct but complementary skill sets. You may
argue that other skills belong on this list as well, but you can't

legitimately claim that we're well equipped if any of these skills are lacking.

In his classic text about scientific research, W. I. B. Beveridge wrote:

> *Successful scientists have often been people with wide interests. Their originality may have derived from their diverse knowledge.*[3]

I agree and believe that this is also true of information professionals. Broad interests and studies tend to produce the best thinkers. Information professionals must expand their minds.

The Root of the Problem

We face a fundamental problem today. Most people who work as information professionals—those on whom organizations rely for deriving understanding from data—have been trained solely in the use of one or more data analysis tools and have not developed the other skills listed above. Most data analysis tools aren't very good, but even if we've been trained in one of the best, that alone doesn't enable us to derive understanding from data. In fact, training in a tool makes us dangerous if we lack the conceptual skills that are required to use that tool effectively. Tools can't do our thinking for us. No tools can provide or replace the skills that are needed to make sense of data. If we focus only on learning tools, we will fail to develop the conceptual skills that are needed to use those tools effectively.

Moreover, most of the tools that we rely on are so poorly designed that we're forced to spend hour upon hour learning the mechanics of using them. We struggle to find and memorize where functions hide within labyrinthine menu systems. We're forced to learn tricks to work around badly designed or missing features. On top of all this, the tools change so often that, just when we think we've learned enough to get by, the cycle starts all over again. Organizations hiring information professionals typically focus on tools experience rather than essential thinking skills. This naïve approach leads each new generation of information professionals to focus on the least essential skills of tool mastery if they want to get hired. This cycle of dysfunction keeps our profession mired in mediocrity.

The failure of information technology vendors to design good tools keeps us running on a treadmill of wasted effort. If our tools were well designed, they would become invisible. That is, they would become such a natural extension of our thinking, we would almost forget we're using them, and instead we would spend our time thinking with data rather than struggling to get a grip on the clumsy mechanics of using the tools. Good tools, properly used, can complement and enhance our thinking skills but never replace them. We must focus on developing these thinking skills and holding technology vendors responsible for supporting them. Those vendors have led us astray. One of their perpetual marketing messages has been that their "revolutionary" tools will transform us into skilled information professionals. Like snake-oil salesmen of old, they claim, "Just learn our tools and your data will suddenly come alive with meaning." Their emphasis in recent years on *self-service* business intelligence and analytics is an insidious expression of this marketing ruse. Self-service makes sense for activities such as pumping fuel at a gas station or printing travel tickets at an airport kiosk because these activities require minimal skills. Self-service does not make sense for the activities that are required for deriving understanding from data because these activities require a broad array of well-honed skills.

The self-service model is popular because it's convenient. Wouldn't it be nice if we could make sense of data so easily? The truth, however, is that information professionals must work diligently through years of training and practice to develop the required skills. This truth is not at all popular. In fact, it's damned inconvenient, but it's true nonetheless. If we want to use data effectively, if we want to finally usher in an information age worthy of the name, we must commit ourselves to the hard work of skills development. Until we do this, we will remain in a dark age of data confusion.

The Final Straw

I began thinking about this problem seriously in 2015. At the time, I wrote an article titled "A Course of Study in Analytical Thinking" to identify and describe the thinking skills that are needed to make sense of data. I even toyed with the idea of developing and teaching a course to introduce people to this broad range of thinking skills, but I found the logistics challenging. Teaching any one of the skill sets listed above (critical thinking, scientific thinking, etc.) would involve lectures, discussions, and learning activities spread across several weeks. It couldn't be managed in the consecutive days of a multi-day workshop. I shelved the idea at the time, but I never abandoned my concern or interest.

In 2018, an encounter with a client brought the importance of these skills back into focus with considerable force. I was invited to give a keynote presentation about data visualization at an internal analytics event for a large manufacturer of medical devices. I ordinarily turn down invitations to speak at private events, but I care a great deal about health care and knew that this particular company contributed a lot of equipment to the field. Often, when preparing a presentation for a particular organization, I request examples of data visualizations produced by its employees, which I then incorporate into the presentation to personalize it for the audience. In response to my request for examples in this case, I was given information about an internal data visualization competition that the medical device company had recently run, including all of the competitors' submissions. When I reviewed the goal of the competition, along with the data set that was provided to participants, I was puzzled because it was instantly obvious to me that the goal could not possibly be achieved based on the data set. When I went on to review the submissions, my confusion turned into grave concern because every one of the participants had examined the data, formed conclusions, and expressed them as data visualizations even though no reliable conclusions were possible. Every competitor had failed to think critically about the data.

Here's the scenario. The data visualization competition assigned the following objective:

> Based on the data set that has been provided, identify the best sales opportunities for our company's devices for treating strokes.

The data set consisted of the following items:

- Hospital (ID and name)
- Hospital location (latitude and longitude, city, state, and whether urban or rural)
- Total stroke admissions to the hospital (including readmissions) for the year 2015
- Total stroke admissions to the hospital (including readmissions) for the year 2016
- Stroke readmission rate for the year 2016
- Average length of hospital stay in days for stroke admissions during the year 2016

Data was included for approximately 3,400 hospitals throughout the United States and a few U.S. territories.

Imagine that you work for this company and decide to participate in the competition. How would you begin? If you're thinking critically, you would begin by determining what qualifies as a sales opportunity for your company's stroke treatments. To do this, you would need to find out what devices your company offers for the treatment of strokes and what types of strokes those devices treat because not all strokes are the same. A simple web search reveals that there are two basic types of strokes: ischemic strokes, which are caused by clots that block the passage of blood to the brain, and hemorrhagic strokes, which are caused by bleeding in the brain. They are treated quite differently. Learning this would pose a problem because you haven't been told about the devices that your company offers. Despite this problem, assuming that you could somehow identify the number of strokes of the type that your company's devices treat, you might proceed by asking, "What qualifies as a sales opportunity?" After a little thought, and with a little knowledge of sales, you would conclude the following:

> Sales opportunities are hospitals with patients who are suffering from strokes that our devices are designed to treat—*hospitals that don't already purchase those products in adequate supply.*

What I've italicized above is not revealed in the data set. To determine sales opportunities, it's of no real value to identify hospitals that treat strokes if you don't know whether or not those hospitals are already purchasing your company's devices to the extent that those devices are needed. The only correct answer that you could give in response to the competition's objective is that the total number of sales opportunities that the data set could be used to reliably identify is zero—none whatsoever. The question cannot be answered with the data provided. Nonetheless, the contestants produced a broad range of answers, which consisted entirely of nonsense.

Concerned with what I found, I developed a keynote presentation that touched only lightly on data visualization. Instead, I spoke at great length about the importance of thinking critically with data. I took the audience through the critical thinking steps that the competitors should have taken before they derived conclusions from the data and expressed them as data visualizations.

None of these competitors failed because they were dumb. They were probably all above average in intelligence. They all failed for the same simple reason: they were trying to do something that they were never properly trained to do. In his book, *Don't Believe Everything You Think*, Thomas Kida asks:

> *So why do we fall prey to erroneous thinking? Are we stupid? It certainly doesn't seem so! All of us make...mistakes in thinking and deciding..., including highly trained professionals such as doctors, lawyers, and CEOs of major corporations. Instead, two basic reasons come to mind. First, we all have natural tendencies to search for and evaluate evidence in a faulty manner. The reasons for these tendencies range*

from evolutionary considerations to just wanting to simplify the thinking process. Second, critical thinking and decision-making skills, which could counteract our natural tendencies to err, are typically not taught in our schools. Our education system requires courses in English, history, math, and the sciences, but not in critical thinking and decision making. Yet such courses would develop skills that could have a signifi-cant impact on the decisions we face every day in our lives.[4]

As Kida suggests, the failures of the medical device company that I described above were not unusual. In fact, in my experience, this company is typical. Almost every organization that I've observed—and I've observed many that you would expect to be analytically sophisticated, including most of the top high-tech companies in the world—rely primarily on information professionals who have never been trained in the necessary skills. These organizations might have a few individuals and even some small teams of highly trained information professionals, but the vast majority of data analysis on which they rely is done by people who lack the required skills.

This isn't speculation; this problem is very real and the costs are high. Having smart and talented people does not constitute a skilled workforce if those people lack the particular skills that are needed.

The Foundation of Clear Thinking

Even though each of the thinking skills that I've listed in this chapter are integral to this work, I will focus on only two in this book—critical thinking and scientific thinking—because I believe they are perhaps the most essential and valuable. They are closely related, siblings born of philosophy, but not identical. Together, they form the foundation of clear thinking. Given their unique importance, it seems appropriate to dedicate a book solely to these two topics. Besides, a book that tackled all of the skills that are needed to make sense of data would be rather long.

Data Sensemaking

One last item before we proceed. Throughout this book I will refer to the activities that we engage in to understand quantitative data as *data sensemaking*. By data sensemaking, I simply mean figuring things out, developing understanding, based on data. Many terms have been used to describe this work, including *data analysis, statistics, business intelligence*, and *data science*, but they are all encumbered to some degree with distracting baggage. The term *data analysis* suggests that the process consists entirely of breaking information down into its component parts—digging into the details—which is what analysis means, but this is only one of the activities required to make sense of data. The term *statistics* suggests that the process consists primarily of mathematics, which is not the case. The subset of mathematics formally known as statistics is certainly required, but making sense of data involves much broader thinking. The term *business intelligence*, even though it was originally defined in 1958 by Hans Peter Luhn as "the ability to apprehend interrelationships of presented facts in such a way as to guide action" and later in 1989 by Howard Dresner as "concepts and methods to improve decision-making using fact-based support systems," is popularly understood by most people to mean little more than the production of reports. Besides, this work is not limited to the realm of business, so the term *business intelligence* is unnecessarily restrictive. The term *data science* is an unfortunate misnomer. There are many uses of data in science, but there is no science of data. Data, in and of itself, is not the subject matter of a particular scientific domain, nor do most people who call themselves data scientists apply the scientific method. Unlike all of the above terms, *data sensemaking* has not accumulated confusing baggage—not yet, at least—and it more directly and clearly describes the nature of the work. It is, simply stated, the process of making sense of data.

If we present data without processing it first, we are not involved in data sensemaking, but we are nevertheless influencing the thinking of those who use the information we present. Selecting a particular data set and presenting it to others creates a frame within which they will weave a story. Stories are not necessarily true. When data sensemaking is done without the necessary skills, stories are often little more than imaginative fabrications. All of us who present data to others should be skilled in data sensemaking.

Let's begin to construct a loom that can be used to weave data into something meaningful and useful by learning to think critically and scientifically with data. As you read through the remainder of this book, I suggest that you frequently *pause, take a moment, and think*. One of the biggest obstacles to critical and scientific thinking with data is failing to take our time. Just as it takes a skilled weaver time to make a sturdy, beautiful textile, it takes time to think critically and scientifically.

CHAPTER 2 – THINK CRITICALLY

Thinking critically does not mean thinking negatively—at least not in this context. To think critically is to think clearly and logically to understand things as they are. The American philosopher, psychologist, and educator, John Dewey (1859-1952) is widely credited as the father of modern *critical thinking*, although he called it by a different name: *reflective thinking*. His definition still stands as one of the best:

> *Active, persistent, and careful consideration of a belief or*
> *supposed form of knowledge in the light of the grounds which*
> *support it and the further conclusions to which it tends.[1]*

Critical thinking is *active*, not passive. We don't just accept beliefs or knowledge as given; we think things through for ourselves. Critical thinking is *persistent*: we must work hard at it and stick to the task. Critical thinking is *careful*: getting things right matters greatly. Critical thinking focuses on the *grounds* that support valid beliefs and knowledge: reason and evidence.

A more recent definition was offered in 1993 by the educators Richard Paul, Alec Fisher, and Gerald Nosich:

> *Critical thinking is that mode of thinking—about any*
> *subject, content or problem—in which the thinker improves*
> *the quality of his or her thinking by skillfully taking charge of*
> *the structures inherent in thinking and imposing standards*
> *upon them.[2]*

We think constantly but seldom critically. Paul, Fisher, and Nosich's definition highlights the importance of becoming conscious of how our minds work and of managing tendencies that interfere with our ability to understand things as they are. To think critically, we must learn to not only recognize reasoning errors but to develop the discipline and skills that are required to avoid these errors.

Critical thinking does not require exceptional intelligence or an advanced academic degree. Anyone can learn to think critically. Relatively few, even among the exceptionally intelligent and highly educated, however, have cultivated critical thinking skills. This is a travesty and the world is paying dearly for it.

Attributes of Critical Thinking

In their foundational textbook on the topic, *Critical Thinking: Tools for Taking Charge of Your Learning and Your Life*,[3] Richard Paul and Linda Elder identify several attributes of critical thinking:

Clarity
Critical thinking is intelligible, easy to understand, and coherent.

Accuracy
To be accurate is to represent something correctly, in accordance with the way it actually is. A statement can be clear, yet inaccurate.

Precision
Precision is exactness. A statement can be both clear and accurate, yet imprecise. "Sales increased tremendously this month" might be clear and accurate, but it's definitely not precise. When we're precise, we express the level of detail that's needed to understand something. If we're vague, our audience can't truly understand what we mean or evaluate the soundness of our conclusions. How helpful is it to upper management to know that there has been a "large gain" in complaints about one of our products? "Large gain" must be precisely defined for someone to know the scale and nature of the problem and be able to devise a plan to remedy it.

Relevance
Something is relevant when it is directly connected with and bears upon the issue at hand. It can be tempting to introduce irrelevant information just because we happen to have it. Irrelevant data, however, is noise.

Depth
Deep thinking goes beneath the surface of an issue or problem, identifies the complexities inherent in it, and then deals with those complexities in an intellectually responsible way.

Breadth
We think broadly when we consider the issue at hand from every relevant perspective.

Logicalness
Logical thinking is coherent. We make a case by combining statements of fact that support one another.

Significance
Critical thinking focuses on what matters. Thinking suffers when we fail to recognize that, although many things may be relevant to an issue, it does not follow that all are equally important.

Now that we've considered critical thinking in general, let's turn to the heart of this chapter—effective reasoning, the process of drawing conclusions from evidence, which in our case means drawing conclusions from data and the context in which the data resides. We'll begin with the ways that reasoning can go astray.

Faulty Reasoning

What inhibits our ability to think critically? The human brain is extraordinary—"a wonder to behold"—but it's the product of natural selection, not of a skilled designer. Natural selection doesn't always produce the best designs. Although the brain's unique evolution has given us an extraordinary ability to reason, the brain has also developed a host of flaws that lead to reasoning errors. Fortunately, thanks in part to recent advances in psychology and neuroscience, many of these flaws have been identified and can, with effort, be avoided. Cognitive biases and logical fallacies are two sides of the same coin; that is, logical fallacies are expressions of cognitive biases. They both interfere with our ability to think critically, so we will consider them in an integrated manner.

Two Modes of Thinking—System 1 and System 2

There are many ways to categorize the human brain's fundamental abilities and modes of operation. One that is especially useful for our purposes was popularized by the behavioral psychologist Daniel Kahneman who speaks of two fundamental modes of thinking—*System 1* and *System 2*. Others have proposed similar models using different terms, but we'll stick with Kahneman's language to keep things simple. The best resource for learning about this is Kahneman's excellent book *Thinking, Fast and Slow*.

System 1 is the more ancient of the two modes. It's fast, intuitive, and often emotional. System 2, which emerged with the development of the brain's pre-frontal cortex, is slower, more reflective, and more rational. Most human thinking is of the System 1 type. This is appropriate, for System 1 does a good job of handling most of the situations that we face in everyday life. Our brains process information and make decisions constantly, quickly, and to a large degree unconsciously to get us through the day. System 1 thinking doesn't require attention. System 1 often fails us, however, when we deal with novel situations that require reflection or any situations that require deeper, more rational thinking. According to Kahneman,

> *System 1 is generally very good at what it does: its models of familiar situations are accurate, its short-term predictions are usually accurate as well, and its initial reactions to challenges are swift and generally appropriate. System 1 has*

*biases, however, systematic errors that it is prone to make in
specified circumstances…It sometimes answers easier
questions than the one it was asked, and it has little
understanding of logic and statistics.*[4]

*System 2 is the only one that can follow rules, compare
objects on several attributes, and make deliberate choices
between options. The automatic System 1 does not have
these capabilities. System 1 detects simple relations ("they
are all alike," "the son is much taller than the father") and
excels at integrating information about one thing, but it does
not deal with multiple distinct topics at once, nor is it adept
at using purely statistical information…A crucial capability
of System 2 is the adoption of "task sets": it can program
memory to obey an instruction that overrides habitual
responses.*[5]

System 1 acts on simple rules of thumb, called *heuristics*. These
heuristics work fine when we are dealing with ordinary situations
but often don't work when we face unfamiliar or complex situations. "When faced with a difficult question, we often answer an
easier one instead, usually without noticing the substitution."[6] For
example, if we were asked, "What occurs more often, deaths from
shark attacks or from falling airplane parts?" most of us would pick
shark attacks as the seemingly obvious answer, not because of
relevant statistical information, but because we hear about shark
attacks more often. In other words, rather than answering the
question that was asked, we would answer the easier question,
"What cause of death have you heard about more often: shark
attacks or falling airplane parts?" The answer to the easier question
is not always the correct answer to the question that was asked.
Statistically, falling airplane parts cause more deaths than shark
attacks.

We can only do a good job of making many of the decisions that
we face in the complex modern world that we've created by asking
the right questions and shifting into System 2 thinking to answer
them. System 1 heuristics are also known as *cognitive biases*: a

tendency to see things in a particular way without reflecting on the facts. Making decisions based on those biases can produce unintended and undesirable results. No degree of intelligence eliminates our susceptibility to cognitive biases. Cognitive biases are not a sign of stupidity but remnants of behaviors that worked admirably in our ancestral environment. That environment has now largely vanished, however, and the biases that we developed to survive in it do not always serve us well today.

Fortunately, we can learn to identify our cognitive biases and then avoid them. This process is simple in concept but requires more energy, which our brains are not inclined to expend, because we're inclined to be lazy—to seek the System 1 path of least effort. When faced with the errors of System 1 thinking, we must slow down and shift into the harder work of System 2 thinking.

We can improve our data-sensemaking abilities by learning to identify cognitive biases and the logical fallacies that they produce. This involves *metacognition*—thinking about thinking. The more we think about thinking—how thinking works and the ways in which it's often flawed—the better we are able to work around its limitations.

Descriptions and Arguments

As data sensemakers, we describe what we observe in data and sometimes draw conclusions from those observations based on arguments. Descriptions present what is happening. We observe what's going on in the data and present what we find to those who might benefit from that information. Much of our work involves descriptions. Arguments go further than descriptions by drawing conclusions from premises. Arguments also often suggest courses of action.

There are two logical forms of argument: *deduction* and *induction*. The conclusions that we assert in arguments, whether deductive or inductive, are based on premises—statements of fact. Deductive arguments strive to establish that something specific is certain based on general premises that are certain. Inductive arguments, in contrast, strive to establish that something general is highly probable rather than certain, based on multiple specific examples that serve as the argument's premises.

A deductive argument is said to be *valid* if the premises logically support the conclusion. In a validly constructed deduction, if the premises are true, then the conclusion must also be true. If one or more of the premises are not true, however, a deductive argument could still be valid (internally consistent), but it would be *unsound* because the facts are wrong.

The Greek philosopher Aristotle provided the most familiar example of a valid deductive argument, constructed in the form of a *syllogism*:

> *Socrates is a man.*
> *All men are mortal.*
> *Therefore, Socrates is mortal.*

The first two lines are the premises, and the final line is the conclusion. Both premises are assumed to be certain. The conclusion follows logically from the premises.

And here is Aristotle's classic example of an invalid deductive argument:

> *Coriscus is different from Socrates.*
> *Socrates is a man.*
> *Therefore, Coriscus is not a man.*

Coriscus may differ from Socrates in many ways other than by not being a man. For instance, one obvious way that Coriscus differs from Socrates is that few of us know of him while Socrates is well known. (In case you're wondering, he was one of Aristotle's buddies when he attended Plato's Academy.) It does not follow logically from the premises that Coriscus is not a man.

When we reason inductively rather than deductively, we do not assume that our premises are certain—true in all cases. Whereas "All men are mortal" is assumed to be certain, "Every man that I know loves sports" admits the possibility of exceptions. Love of sports among men is likely—probable to some degree—but not certain. Inductive arguments determine probable conclusions based on probable evidence.

> *John loves to watch football.*
> *Harold loves to watch football.*
> *Gary loves to watch football.*
> *Men love to watch football.*

Whereas a deductive argument done properly is said to be *valid*, an inductive argument done properly is said to be *strong*. Unlike deductive arguments, which are either valid or not, inductive arguments vary in strength based on the preponderance of evidence. In the case above, examples of three men who love to watch football do not provide enough evidence to conclude that all men love football.

As Hugh G. Gauch, Jr. says of deduction and induction, "They pursue answers to different kinds of questions, with deduction reasoning from a mental model to expected data, and induction reasoning from actual data to a mental model."[7] Although deductive and inductive arguments are equally important, inductive arguments are more prevalent in data sensemaking. We are most often looking at actual data and trying to explain what the data means.

In addition to deduction and induction, there is another valid and useful form of argument: *abduction*. Even though it isn't formally classified as a logical form of argument, it's the primary form of reasoning that's used in science, as we'll see in the next chapter. Sean Carroll describes abduction in his book *The Big Picture*:

> *Whenever we are confronted with questions about belief, we can employ the technique called abduction, or "inference to the best explanations." Abduction is a type of reasoning that can be contrasted with deduction and induction. With deduction, we start with some axioms whose truth we do not question, and derive rigorously necessary conclusions from them. With induction, we start with some examples we know about, and generalize to a wider context—rigorously, if we*

> *have some reason for believing that such a generalization is*
> *always correct, but often we don't quite have that guarantee.*
> *With abduction, by contrast, we take all of our background*
> *knowledge about how the world works, and perhaps some*
> *preference for simple explanations over complex ones..., and*
> *decide what possible explanation provides the best account of*
> *all the facts we have.[8]*

Similar to induction, abduction deals in probabilities, not certainties. We begin with a tentative conclusion based on what we already know and then adjust it as each new piece of evidence emerges. A formulaic and quantitative version of abduction—*Bayesian statistics*—was proposed in the 18th century by Thomas Bayes, a British mathematician and Presbyterian minister. Once again, Carrol provides a useful explanation:

> *Bayes's main idea, now known simply as Bayes's Theorem, is*
> *a way to think about credences* [degrees of belief]. *It allows*
> *us to answer the following question. Imagine that we have*
> *certain credences assigned to different beliefs. Then we gather*
> *some information, and learn something new. How does that*
> *new information change the credences we have assigned?*
> *That's the question we need to be asking ourselves over and*
> *over, as we learn new things about the world.[9]*

In other words, Bayes's Theorem helps us quantitatively update our picture of how the world works to account for the new information.

> *Bayes's Theorem can be thought of as a quantitative version*
> *of the method of... "abduction." (Abduction places emphasis*
> *on finding the "best explanation," rather than just fitting the*
> *data, but methodologically the ideas are quite similar.) It's*
> *the basis of all science and other forms of empirical*
> *reasoning. It suggests a universal scheme for thinking about*
> *our degrees of belief: start with some prior credences, then*
> *update them when new information comes in, based on the*
> *likelihood of that information being compatible with each*
> *original possibility.[10]*

Bayesian statistics is beyond the scope of this book, but I recommend that you become familiar with its methods.

Deductive arguments can be valid and both inductive and abductive arguments can be strong, but they are all unsound if their premises aren't accurate. Premises are based on facts, and in all forms of argument, we must get our facts right. We'll consider the importance of the facts—metrics in particular—in "Chapter 5 – Measure Wisely." For now, we'll focus on errors in reasoning that we must avoid to reach reliable conclusions.

Common Reasoning Errors in Data Sensemaking

Whether we're providing descriptions or making arguments, our reasoning can suffer from errors. Reasoning errors can be categorized in many ways. For our purposes, as we focus on data sensemaking, I've grouped them as follows:

- Familiarity errors
- Statistical errors
- Causal errors

We'll examine the reasoning errors in each of these three categories in turn. I'll introduce each error by first illustrating it with a practical example.

Familiarity Errors

All of the errors in this category rely on understanding that is assumed merely because the information on which it's based is in some manner familiar. We are naturally biased to accept answers that are familiar. Truth is not always contained in the familiar, however.

Confirmation Bias

> As an avid supporter of the Second Amendment, I pay a lot of attention to news stories about shootings, and I can tell you that there's no point in passing additional anti-gun legislation. In every shooting I can think of, the guns were

obtained illegally, so legislation wouldn't make a difference. I
wrote about this recently on a gun-enthusiast message board
that I frequent and received a flood of responses from people
who cited new stories about shooters that acquired their guns
illegally.

This well-known bias is the tendency to search for, interpret, focus on, and remember information in a way that confirms our existing beliefs. We confirm what we believe to be true by seeking and noticing information that supports it and by ignoring information that doesn't. We usually do this unconsciously, and, unless we're careful, routinely.

Confirmation bias does no harm when our beliefs match reality, but it hides the truth when our beliefs are invalid. Even when our beliefs are based on a great deal of thinking in the past, we dare not embrace them with certainty. It's appropriate to hold tightly to well-formed beliefs by being suspicious of information that conflicts with them, but not so tightly that we ignore conflicting evidence. Thomas Huxley once said:

> *My business is to teach my aspirations to conform themselves*
> *to fact, not to try to make facts harmonize with my aspira-*
> *tions. Sit down before fact as a little child, be prepared to give*
> *up every preconceived notion, follow humbly wherever nature*
> *leads, or you will learn nothing.*[11]

Every encounter with data that conflicts with our beliefs gives us an opportunity to revise them, and in doing so, to improve our understanding.

Selective perception is another name for instances of confirmation bias that work at the level of perception. From a vast array of available information, we selectively attend only to that which matches our beliefs. If we expect to find a particular answer in the data, we'll only notice data consistent with that answer.

We can combat biases of this type by identifying our expectations and consciously setting them aside. To make sense of data, we must open ourselves to the possibility of being surprised by new information that doesn't match our expectations.

There's a subtle version of confirmation bias that doesn't necessarily require a prior belief that something is true. Whenever we generate a hypothesis, such as the proposition that an increase in the number of clicks on a product's web page results in a corresponding increase in the number of sales, we tend to automatically want it to be true, simply because it's ours, so we seek to confirm it. To some degree this tendency is driven by ego; it seeks to affirm our positive self-image. It's also easier than generating and testing several hypotheses, but truth isn't always convenient, and it certainly isn't always contained in the first hypothesis that we generate.

Availability Heuristic

> *What is the capital city of Illinois? Chicago, right?*

Actually, Springfield is the capital of Illinois, but the city of Chicago is more familiar to most of us. Ask most people to name a city in Illinois other than Chicago and they'll struggle to come up with one. The *availability heuristic* latches onto the answer that most readily comes to mind—the one that is most available—not necessarily the right answer.

If we're examining data to determine why sales increased during the month of December, we might be tempted to give credit to the marketing campaign that occurred in that month with great fanfare simply because it's the explanation that most readily comes to mind. The actual answer, however, could be that sales always go up in December because the sales team earns great bonuses by closing sales before the end of the year, but that's less familiar and would require some research into factors other than the obvious marketing campaign.

Instances of the availability heuristic are sometimes called the *mere exposure effect*. Here's an example:

> *Humans only use 10% of their brains. We've all heard this many times, so it must be true.*

The more that we're exposed to something, the more available it becomes to our memories, and the more it seems to be true. It's hard to distinguish truth from what's merely familiar through consistent and frequent exposure. We've all heard that we humans only use 10% of our brains. We've heard it many times, but it isn't true. We humans use 100% of our brains. How well we use them differs, but we use them entirely. So, how did this erroneous statement of fact become well known and assumed to be true? Someone made this statement in an article long ago and others have quoted it ever since, almost never questioning its validity. It seems true only because it's familiar through frequent use. In the business of data sensemaking, we should make it our practice to ask whether we have seen proof of the things we "know" from familiar exposure but haven't actually verified. Proof can be in the form of evidence, data, a well-supported and explained argument by an expert using the principles of abductive reasoning that we discussed above, or other similar logical and verifiable justifications.

Status Quo Bias

> *We've always increased revenues by establishing targets for salespeople that are 10% above their sales in the previous year. There's no need to question this time-honored approach.*

We take comfort in what's already established. We tend to prefer that things remain the same. In other words, we are biased toward the status quo. This holds true for our understanding of things as well. Once we think we understand something, we tend to hold tightly to it. What's familiar isn't always true, however. The truth, even when it's unfamiliar, is more useful than a well-established fiction. As data sensemakers, we should question what we've always done or thought and approach each new question or problem with fresh eyes.

Default Effect

> *The default method for dealing with cost overruns is to downsize. Let's respond to current cost overruns by deter-mining the number of employees that must be laid off to bring our actual expenses back into line with the budget.*

This is similar to the status quo bias—a standard response that doesn't necessarily take the specifics of a situation or problem into account. Sometimes in life, particular choices are established as defaults to make them convenient, to nudge us in their direction. For most people most of the time, defaults are good enough. We rarely consider other, less convenient options. For example, software applications establish particular choices as the defaults. The declared intention of software designers is to make the choices that, in their opinion, most often work best, the choices that are most convenient. This is intended to save us time and effort. Defaults are not always the best choices and should not be accepted without question, however, especially when we're trying to make sense of data. We should consider all options before accepting a default, and even after a default has been consciously established, we should question its appropriateness in each novel situation.

The default effect can hamper data sensemaking in two ways. First, it encourages us to go through the exact same steps in the exact same way every time we approach the data. Following the same path will usually lead us to the same destination. Different paths can provide perspectives that broaden and deepen our understanding. Second, the default effect is in play when we accept particular answers to questions simply because they're answers that have always been assumed rather than answers that resulted from examining the data. Default answers can be wrong and often are. Sometimes default answers were true at one time but conditions changed, rendering them invalid. In some cases the default answer was never correct. Data sensemakers should always question and investigate the validity of a default choice or method to determine whether it applies to the specific situation at hand.

Anchoring Effect

> *My sales analyst, Thomas, predicts that sales this year will reach $982,000. This seems slightly high to me, so I'll reduce the forecast to $975,000.*

This bias occurs when estimating values. If we have a particular number in mind before estimating a value, our estimate tends to remain near that number. The number that was originally proposed serves as an anchor, keeping subsequent estimates in the vicinity. As an example, the anchoring effect has been shown to heavily influence estimates of home values that are made by professional appraisers when they have been informed in advance of the buyer's offer. The amount of the offer serves as a powerful anchor that appraisers often match precisely or nearly so.

I experienced a common example of the anchoring effect while admiring paintings at an art gallery recently. The gallery owner mistook my lingering glance at a painting of partially used crayons arranged in the shape of a peace sign as interest. Although the price tag stated $2,100, the owner quickly offered to discount the price to $1,800—a frequent and often successful ploy. A price of $1,800 seems like a great bargain compared to the original price of $2,100, but without that anchor, even $1,800 would probably seem like a lot of money for a painting of crayons.

If we're asked to estimate, predict, or forecast a value, and we know that a particular value is desired or expected, we will be inclined to keep our estimate within close proximity. The best way to avoid the anchoring effect is to have no values in mind in advance. When a value has already been inserted into our consciousness, we should intentionally work to set it aside.

Semmelweis Effect

> It is obvious that large, heavy objects fall faster than small, light objects. Galileo's experiment must be flawed.

Knowledge resides in our brains in the form of *mental models*. These models (a.k.a., *paradigms*) can be wrong. If they are built upon solid reason and evidence, they are less likely to be wrong than those that are built using methods and data that are shoddy, but we still shouldn't mistake them for certainty. The *Semmelweis effect* is the tendency to reject new evidence that contradicts an existing paradigm. "I'll see it when I believe it." Seeing only what fits our existing paradigms comes naturally.

One of the great tenets of the scientific method is that existing explanations are never inviolable but remain open to revision when new evidence is found that calls them into question. This is how science advances. Likewise, this is how understanding in all realms progresses.

Appeal to Common Belief

> *The world is flat. Everyone knows this.*

The claim that most or many people accept something as true exercises a great deal of influence over us. However, history makes it clear that many common beliefs about the world have been wrong. Everyone believing something doesn't make it true. We can't accept the commonality of a belief as evidence of its truth.

This bias is closely related to a long list of related biases with names that all begin with "appeal to" and base the appeal on something other than a reasonable assessment of the evidence. For example, the following statement illustrates the *appeal to common sense*:

> *Time is immutable. That's just common sense. It would be ridiculous to believe that time runs at different rates in different places.*

Other biases of this type include:

- *appeal to authority* (i.e., someone with authority makes the claim, so it must be true)
- *appeal to accomplishment* (i.e., someone who is accomplished makes the claim, so it must be true)
- *appeal to consequences* (i.e., it must be true because it's desirable)
- *appeal to desperation* (i.e., it must be true because something must be done, and this solution is better than nothing)
- *appeal to emotion* (i.e., it must be true because of something the audience cares about, fears, etc.)

- *appeal to intuition* (i.e., it must be true because I have a gut feeling that it is)
- *appeal to nature* (i.e., it must be true because it's natural)
- *appeal to trust* (i.e., it must be true because the source is trustworthy)

The complete list is longer, but you get the idea.

Law of the Instrument

> *Excel provides the best means to analyze data. Sticking to the methods that Excel provides is the right approach.*

This final reasoning error we'll consider that conflates truth with familiarity is our tendency to trust and therefore heavily rely on the methods that are provided by familiar tools, ignoring or undervaluing alternative approaches. As the common expression goes, if your only tool (or your favorite tool) is a hammer, everything will look like a nail. This is a pervasive problem in data sensemaking. We tend to rely on one or two tools, learn the methods that those tools support, and never deviate from them. Those tools and methods powerfully frame the way that we see and approach the data. If we have a data visualization tool, we tend to rely exclusively on graphs. Even worse, we tend to rely solely on the charts that the tool features, rarely questioning their appropriateness for the task at hand. If we suddenly became the happy recipients of a new machine learning tool, we might begin to see every data-sensemaking problem as one that should be addressed by using machine learning algorithms. People sometimes spend days figuring out how to apply machine learning algorithms to do what could be done in a matter of minutes by merely using their eyes to examine the data in a few simple charts.

Unfortunately, most of us have developed our data-sensemaking skills almost entirely by learning particular tools. This approach cuts us off from learning the basic concepts and practices that must be in place before we can use any tools effectively. As a result, those tools become our hammers, making all problems look like nails, so we merrily pound the data into submission. A skilled carpenter uses a broad assortment of tools. Carpenters learn the properties of the materials that they work with and the qualities of fine construction before they select particular tools. Data sensemakers must do the same.

As you have probably noticed, all of these biases that are fueled by familiarity are quite similar. We can address all of them with one broad stroke by recognizing that what's familiar or seemingly established, for whatever reason, is not necessarily true. We add no value as data sensemakers if we mindlessly conflate familiarity with truth. If our brains couldn't think beyond the familiar to see things differently, we humans would still be hanging out in trees on the African savannah. To overcome familiarity errors, we must consciously shift into System 2 thinking to question data more broadly, deeply, and carefully.

Statistical Errors

Many of the errors that we make in data sensemaking are statistical in nature. Statistical thinking does not come naturally to any of us. We must learn to recognize routine statistical errors and how to avoid them.

Law of Small Numbers

> To date, eight people have been diagnosed with the new strain of the disease. Most of the patients have been Hispanic men. From this we can conclude that Hispanic men are more susceptible to the disease than other groups.

This cognitive bias leads us to believe that observations made when examining a small number of instances represent the general nature or routine behavior of something. This is also called the *hasty generalization error*. It's a common problem, even in scientific research. Kahneman has this to say about it:

> A strong bias toward believing that small samples closely resemble the population from which they were drawn is also part of a larger story: we are prone to exaggerate the consis-

tency and coherence of what we see. The exaggerated faith of researchers in what can be learned from a few observations is closely related to the halo effect, the sense we often get that we know and understand a person about whom we actually know very little. System 1 runs ahead of the facts in constructing a rich image on the basis of scraps of evidence.[12]

Particular observations, however true, do not necessarily apply to all cases. We get into trouble when we generalize based on an insufficient number of observations or on observations that only apply to specific situations.

Another closely related error in logic is called the *biased sample fallacy*. This occurs when we draw a conclusion about an entire population based on a small data sample that we selected to make it appear that the population in general matches a particular profile. This is also an example of the fallacy called *cherry picking.* We can easily make the data say anything we want by carefully selecting— consciously or unconsciously—only those records that support our case.

Properly selected samples can indeed tell us a great deal about the overall nature of a population. The key is to learn how to select samples that represent the population. The instances that we include in a sample should be randomly selected from the entire population over an adequate period of time. If we want to under-stand sales performance across an entire year based on a sample, we would need to select instances from every part of the year to represent the full spectrum of behavior.

We sometimes also need to restrict the scope of the population that we're interested in understanding to a homogeneous group. For example, if we want to understand the heights of fire fighters, we should narrow the scope of the population either to men or to women, for these two groups differ significantly in average height. Statistical descriptions of populations that combine distinct groups that differ significantly in relation to the trait of interest are of little value. The resulting statistic (e.g., average height of a population that includes both men and women) does not characterize any of the groups.

Insensitivity to Sample Size

> *Small rural hospitals take much longer than other hospitals*
> *to treat stroke patients. All of the hospitals with the highest*
> *average length of stay for stroke treatment fall into this*
> *category. Small rural hospitals should therefore be motivated*
> *to improve their ability to treat strokes efficiently.*

This is the tendency to misinterpret variation in small samples as
relatively excessive. Unless we've studied statistics beyond the mere
basics, we're not likely to realize that small data sets often exhibit
more variation on average than large data sets. Consider statistics
related to the average lengths of stay for stroke treatment in two
hospitals: one small and one large. The small hospital, due to its
size, treats far fewer stroke patients than the large hospital. Imagine
that in a particular year the small hospital treated 5 stroke patients
while the large hospital treated 100. The number of days that the
five stroke patients remained in the small hospital were as follows,
arranged in order of size:

1, 2, 4, 5, and 25.

No two values are the same. There appears to be a great deal of
variation. Contrast this with the following values for the large
hospital:

1, 1, 1, 1, 1, 1, 1, 1, 1, 1, 1, 1, 1, 1, 1, 1, 1, 1, 1, 1, 1, 1, 1, 1,
1, 2, 2, 2, 2, 2, 2, 2, 2, 2, 2, 2, 2, 2, 2, 2, 2, 2, 2, 2, 2, 2, 2, 2,
2, 2, 2, 2, 2, 2, 2, 3, 3, 3, 3, 3, 3, 3, 3, 3, 3, 3, 3, 3, 3, 3, 3,
3, 3, 3, 3, 3, 3, 3, 3, 3, 3, 3, 3, 3, 3, 4, 4, 4, 4, 4, 4, 4, 4, 5,
5, 5, 6, 6, 10, 15, 25.

Many of the values are the same, so variation appears to be less.
Notice, however, that lengths of stay in both hospitals ranged from
1 to 25 days. If we randomly selected five patients who were treated
at the large hospital, their lengths of stay might precisely match
those of the five who were treated at the small hospital. If we

summarized these two sets of values as the average length of stay for each hospital, based on the mean, the values would be 7.4 for the small hospital versus 2.81 days for the large hospital. The 25-day length of stay outlier would have a great deal of influence on the small hospital's mean but relatively little on that of the large hospital. Furthermore, if we summarized the amount of variation by using the standard deviation, the values would be 9.96 for the small hospital versus 2.91 for the large hospital. It's likely that, if we collected more values for the small hospital, such as for 10 years rather than 1, we would find that its variation would look a lot more like that of the large hospital.

When we compare measures of something among samples that vary significantly in size, including especially small samples, we must take into account that we might not have enough values in those small samples to make meaningful comparisons.

Base Rate Fallacy

> *Most applicants to Harvard University are rejected. I won't be rejected, however, because I'm really smart.*

This is the error of ignoring what usually happens—the base rate—when determining the likelihood of a particular outcome. There are sometimes good reasons to expect outcomes that are different from the norm, but we should still take the base rate into account first and then make adjustments up or down from there. Most people who apply to Harvard University are really smart, yet most are not accepted. One would need to be more than just "really smart" to expect acceptance.

It's easy to screw up when comparing the likelihood of various outcomes. Let me illustrate. Read the following paragraph about a fellow named George:

> *If you meet George, you aren't likely to forget him. Although insecure as a child, George learned that he could get people to like him by being the class clown. An imaginative kid, he was always coming up with new and creative ways to entertain*

people. As he grew into adulthood, he continued to seek experiences that put him in the spotlight.

Now, given this information, rank the following four statements about George in terms of their likelihood:

- George works in finance.
- George is a professional actor.
- George loves jazz music.
- George is a professional actor who loves jazz music.

Before moving on, be sure to assign a number from one through four to each of these statements to rank their likelihood.

Did you rank "George is a professional actor" and "George is a professional actor who loves jazz music" as your top two choices? If so, you've ignored the base rate. If you think about it more carefully, you'll realize that far more people work in finance than as professional actors. Given this fact, it's far more likely that George works in finance than as an actor. If you made this error, you were unduly influenced by the fact that George's personality fits characteristics that we tend to associate with actors, overshadowing the greater relevance of the base rate. None of the hints into his personality in the paragraph above should encourage us to set the base rate aside, and none are inconsistent with a job in finance.

Let's consider another example—one that confirms the importance of the base rate when dealing with probabilities, which are often unintuitive. Imagine that your doctor had you take a blood test to see if you have a particular disease that affects 1 in 10,000 people. The test is 99% effective: only 1% of the time does it fail to identify someone who has the disease (a false negative result) and only 1% of the time does it indicate that someone has the disease who doesn't (a false positive result). When the test results are in, you receive the dreaded news that, according to the test, you have the disease. Given the test's accuracy, what is the likelihood that you actually have the disease? Before reading further, pick a percentage that expresses the probability that you have the disease?

If you're like most people, you believe there is a 99% probability that you have the disease and a 1% probability that you don't have it. Would it shock you to learn that you have the right percentages, but have them backwards? In fact, there is only a 1% probability that you have the disease. To understand this, you must start by considering the base rate. In this scenario, the base rate is the probability of 1 in 10,000 that you have the disease. The fact that the test falsely identifies 1% of people as having the disease—that's 1 out of 100—indicates that out of 10,000 people who are tested, it produces false positives for 100 people. So, if 10,000 are tested, on average 1 will be correctly identified as having the disease and 100 will be incorrectly identified as having it, so the likelihood that you actually have the disease is 1 out of 101, which is slightly less than 1%. Thinking about probabilities can be tricky. Even most medical doctors—the folks who give us the results of tests like this—don't understand how to interpret them.

As data sensemakers, we should become familiar with base rates and keep them firmly in mind when determining the likelihood of particular outcomes.

Hot-Hand Fallacy

> Each of John's last four shots in the basketball game were successful. He's clearly on a roll. His next shot will likely make it as well.

This is the tendency to overestimate the importance of small runs, streaks, or clusters in random data. Many gamblers are susceptible to this bias, assuming that a streak of luck—the product of chance—will continue.

This is an example of a broader tendency to see meaningful patterns in random events. Thomas Gilovich points out that this problem has long been recognized.

> In 1677, Baruch Spinoza wrote his famous words, "Nature abhors a vacuum," to describe a host of physical phenomena. Three hundred years later, it seems that his statement applies as well to human nature, for it too abhors a vacuum. We are predisposed to see order, pattern, and meaning in the world, we find randomness, chaos, and meaninglessness

unsatisfying. Human nature abhors a lack of predictability
and the absence of meaning. As a consequence, we tend to
"see" order where there is none, and we spot meaningful
patterns where only the vagaries of chance are operating.[13]

Bad decisions are frequently made when we endow random events
with illusory meaning and significance. People sometimes lose their
jobs because something in their sphere of responsibility went
poorly entirely by chance. As data sensemakers, we must understand what causes the outcomes that we observe in data and
distinguish those that are random from those that result from
identifiable causes. Only when we recognize random events for
what they are can we refrain from investing them with meaning
and wasting time pursuing matters that we can't possibly influence.

Appeal to Coincidence

The fact that many more patients than usual were treated for
respiratory problems today is just a fluke. Poor air quality
probably has nothing to do with it, despite smoke from the
local fires.

This is the opposite of the previous error. It's the tendency to
conclude that something happened due to chance when the
evidence suggests otherwise. Values do vary randomly from the
norm, but we shouldn't assume that significant changes are due to
chance. We should constantly be on the lookout for outliers. When
we spot them, we should neither assume that they're due to chance
nor caused by something in particular. We should investigate. If we
find the cause, we might actually be able to do something about it.

Regression Fallacy

Sally's blood pressure was higher than usual when the nurse
checked it last month, so Sally cut back her salt intake. Her
blood pressure was normal when the nurse checked it today.
Obviously, cutting back on salt did the trick.

This is the tendency to attribute undue meaning and significance to routine variation in the data. We tend to read too much into individual values. Measures routinely vary to some degree, but they tend to do so within a predictable range around the measure's central tendency. A strong day of sales today will likely be followed by weaker, closer to average sales tomorrow. If John scored 24 points in today's basketball game when he only scores 16 points on average, he will probably score fewer points in the next game. Similarly, if he scored only eight points today, he will likely score more points in the next game. This tendency is called *regression to the mean*. Values will typically fall above their central tendency about as often as they fall below it.

The key here is to become familiar with the range of routine behavior and not become overly concerned when values move around within that range. *Statistical Process Control (SPC)* teaches a collection of methods for tracking measures over time to distinguish when they are behaving routinely from occasions when either something unusual has occurred to produce extreme behavior or something in the process has changed to produce a new norm. Every data sensemaker should learn the basics of SPC. The best introduction to the field that I've found is the book *Understanding Variation* by Donald Wheeler. Also, if you're interested in using charts to monitor data using the principles of SPC, I provide instruction in my book *Signal*.

Variation Blindness

> *I've determined that, on average, our customers are 24 years old. I now understand how our customers are characterized by age.*

This is the tendency to develop a narrow understanding of something based solely on a measure of central tendency—an average—without taking into account the extent to which and the manner in which the measure varies. *Variation blindness* is my own name for this fallacy, which, as far as I know, doesn't have an official name. This common error in data sensemaking stems from a lack of statistical training. Understanding variation is central to statistics.

To understand variation, we must consider at least three character-istics of a measure: its central tendency, its spread (i.e., the range from the lowest to highest values), and its shape.

After undergoing a surgical treatment for abdominal mesothe-lioma—an incurable condition—Stephen Jay Gould, an evolu-tionary biologist who taught at Harvard University, asked the surgeon if she could recommend any technical literature about mesothelioma. In a misguided effort to be humane, she told him that there was nothing worth reading. He took it upon himself to research the literature anyway and soon discovered that, on average, people lived only eight months after receiving the diag-nosis. It isn't hard to imagine how Gould felt upon learning this. After getting over the initial shock of this frightening news, however, as a scientist who was trained in statistics, Gould realized that there was more to the story of how long he might live than a measure of central tendency. The eight-month lifespan was the median. In an article titled "The Median Isn't the Message," Gould described his experience:

> I realized with a gulp why my doctor had offered that
> humane advice. The literature couldn't have been more
> brutally clear: mesothelioma is incurable, with a median
> mortality of only eight months after discovery. I sat stunned
> for about fifteen minutes, then smiled and said to myself: so
> that's why they didn't give me anything to read. Then my
> mind started to work again, thank goodness.[14]

After learning the median, Gould went on to find that people with his condition ranged in remaining lifespan from dying immedi-ately to 20 years. In other words, the potential lifespan was a 20-year spread. Next, he wanted to understand the shape of the distribution. By comparing the 8-month median value to the 20-year spread, he determined that the distribution was severely skewed. Finally, he wanted to understand what the people who lived the longest were like, because he wanted to determine whether he might be one of them. With further investigation he found that he had good reason to believe that he might live for many more years. His musings about this encounter with a cold, hard measure of central tendency that was insufficient in and of itself, included the following insights.

> We still carry the historical baggage of a Platonic heritage that seeks sharp essences and definite boundaries...This Platonic heritage, with its emphasis in clear distinctions and separated immutable entities, leads us to view statistical measures of central tendency wrongly, indeed opposite to the appropriate interpretation in our actual world of variation, shadings, and continua. In short, we view means and medians as the hard "realities," and the variation that permits their calculation as a set of transient and imperfect measurements of this hidden essence. If the median is the reality and variation around the median just a device for its calculation, then "I will probably be dead in eight months" may pass as a reasonable interpretation.
>
> Variation itself is nature's only irreducible essence. Variation is the hard reality, not a set of imperfect measures for a central tendency. Means and medians are the abstractions.[15]

Gould went on to live for 20 more years and did some of his best work during the final years of his life.

We dare not read too much into measures of central tendency. We certainly can't rely on them alone. Only when combined with the spread and shape of the distribution can measures of central tendency give us a sense of variation, "nature's only irreducible essence." As Stacey Barr wrote, "Averages only tell a static story, like a photograph; but variability shows a movie."[16] As data sense-makers, we need to review movies.

Almost all of the statistical errors in the list above stem from reading too much into too little. We can overcome these errors by thinking critically, first about the population that we want to understand, to make sure that it's a homogeneous group, and second about the sample, to ensure that it represents that population.

Causal Errors

A great deal of data sensemaking seeks to understand causes. At least it should. Answering the question "What causes this to happen?" is incredibly important, for only when we understand cause and effect can we produce the outcomes that we desire by encouraging the causes of those outcomes. For example, if we know that customer satisfaction increases significantly when call center operators are not given incentives or mandates to keep calls short, then we can revise our call quota policy to reflect this relationship. We can only predict the outcomes of particular actions if we understand the causes of those outcomes. Conducting *what-if analysis* without understanding the causes of the outcomes we desire is a fool's game.

Despite the essential importance of causation to understanding, it's often ignored. In fact, the discipline of statistics was historically shaped as a causality-free enterprise. Thankfully, this began to change in the 1990s with a renewed emphasis on causality and the development of methods that complement traditional statistics in ways that make it possible to ask and answer questions about causation that were previously off limits. Judea Pearl, a computer scientist and winner of the Turing Award, has contributed a great deal to this trend. He's also written an important book about it titled *The Book of Why: The New Science of Cause and Effect.* As Pearl explains,

> *In vain will you search the index of a statistics textbook for an entry on "cause." Students are not allowed to say that X is the cause of Y—only that X and Y are "related" or "associated."*
>
> *Because of this prohibition, mathematical tools to manage causal questions were deemed unnecessary, and statistics focused exclusively on how to summarize data, not on how to interpret it.[17]*

This causality-free legacy has been successfully challenged in the past three decades, resulting in what some call the *Causal Revolution.*

Unfortunately, during the most recent decade many people have retrogressively argued that with *Big Data* we only need to concern ourselves with correlations, not with causes. As Pearl wisely points out, however,

> *We live in an era that presumes Big Data to be the solution to all our problems. Courses in "data science" are proliferating in our universities, and jobs for "data scientists" are lucrative in the companies that participate in the "data economy." But I hope…to convince you that data are profoundly dumb. Data can tell you that people who took a medicine recovered faster than those who did not take it, but they can't tell you why. Maybe those who took the medicine did so because they could afford it and would have recovered just as fast without it.*
>
> *Over and over again, in science and in business, we see situations where mere data aren't enough. Most big-data enthusiasts, while somewhat aware of these limitations, continue to chase after data-centric intelligence, as if we were still in the Prohibition era.*[18]

Furthermore, Pearl makes the important observation that,

> *You are smarter than your data. Data do not understand causes and effects; humans do.*[19]

Figuring out what causes things to happen can be quite complicated, but there are a few straightforward methods that we can follow to avoid common errors. The philosopher John Stuart Mill (1806-1873) did us a favor by identifying several ways to determine causes, now known as *Mill's Methods*. He identified the following methods:

1. *Method of Agreement*

   If multiple occurrences of something have only one relevant factor in common, that factor must be the cause. For instance, if the only relevant common factor among people who are suffering from an outbreak of cholera is drinking from a particular water source, then that water source must be the cause.

2. *Method of Difference*

This method states that if only one relevant factor is both present when something occurs and absent when it does not occur, that factor must be the cause. To find such causes, we look for those factors that differ depending on the occurrence or non-occurrence of something. For example, if you always wake up with a headache after drinking wine the previous evening and never wake up with a headache when you haven't had wine on the previous evening, the wine might indeed be the cause.

3. *Method of Concomitant Variation*

This method looks not just for relevant factors that are either present or absent, but for factors that are closely correlated with the occurrence of the thing that we're investigating. Variation is said to be correlated when increases in one thing occur along with increases in another, and vice versa. For example, if increases in the amount of food that we eat occur along with increases in the amount that we weigh, and vice versa, then food and weight are correlated. As I've already noted, however, we must keep in mind that correlations alone are not sufficient evidence of causation.

Like many good thinking habits, these methods seem obvious upon reflection, but we still often fail to use them. (Note: Mill proposed two additional methods as well. One was the *Joint Method Agreement and Disagreement*, which combines the first two methods above. The other was the *Method of Residues*, which I left off the list because it's more difficult to understand and less useful than the others). Mill's methods are neither complete nor foolproof, but they serve as good working principles. They are incomplete in that they fail to address two typical challenges that we face when looking for causes: 1) making sure that we've identified all potential causes, and 2) the fact that causation is often a complex mixture of multiple factors.

We should bear in mind that it's often easy to miss relevant factors and, as a consequence, falsely assume that the sole factor we've identified is the only relevant factor. Before the English physician Dr. John Snow confirmed that the well on Broad Street in London was the source of a cholera epidemic that occurred in the 17th century, people assumed that miasma—noxious odors in the air—was the sole relevant factor. After all, neighborhoods where people were dying of cholera always smelled bad, so bad air must be the cause—or so they believed. Until it occurred to Snow that the water supply might be the source of cholera, only miasma was considered. We must look vigilantly for all potentially relevant factors. We can dramatically improve our ability to do this in two ways: 1) by developing a great deal of domain knowledge, which will make us aware of a broader range of potential factors, and 2) by always taking time to look beyond the obvious, refusing to complete the list of potential causes too quickly.

When causation is complex, consisting of multiple factors that interact with one another, which is often the case, we must acknowledge that simple thinking won't do. The skills that are required to tackle these complexities draw heavily upon statistics (e.g., *multiple regression analysis*) and *systems theory*, which both fall outside of this book's scope.

Even though causal reasoning can be tricky and complex, we can easily improve our abilities by recognizing and avoiding common errors. Let's consider a few.

Post Hoc Ergo Propter Hoc

> *Sales of widgets increased soon after the launch of our new marketing campaign; therefore, the campaign has succeeded.*

The Latin phrase *post hoc ergo propter hoc* literally means *after this, therefore because of this*. It's the assumption that, because one thing followed another, the subsequent event was caused by first. While it's true that a preceding event might have caused the following event, it isn't necessarily true. A marketing campaign that was launched before an increase in sales could have caused that increase, but something else entirely might have caused it. It's even possible that an increase routinely occurs at that particular time of year.

Spurious Correlation

> *There is a strong correlation between ice cream sales and drownings, therefore the consumption of ice cream must be causing drownings to occur. We can nip this problem in the bud by banning sales of ice cream.*

As every statistics teacher is duty-bound to point out, "Correlation does not imply causation." Two phenomena can be highly correlated without having a direct causal relationship. Most often, when a correlation exists that isn't causal in nature, both phenomena (e.g., ice cream sales and drownings) are caused by another unidentified factor. Correlations of this type are called *spurious correlations*. Increases in ice cream sales and drownings are both correlated to a third variable: high air temperatures. When the weather is hot, people are more likely to eat ice cream and to drown. In this particular case, however, even the heat doesn't cause the drownings. Instead, the high temperatures cause an increase in swimming, which in turn creates more opportunities for drownings to occur. Drownings tend to actually be caused by either poor swimming skills, adverse swimming conditions (e.g., rip tides), or both.

As I mentioned previously, misguided proponents of Big Data have initiated a renewed tendency to look for correlations without concern for causation. Let me use the example above to illustrate this:

> *There is a fairly strong correlation between ice cream sales and drownings. Given the fact that this finding is based on Big Data, there's no reason to understand whether or how ice cream causes drownings. With Big Data, when we spot a*

correlation, we can take advantage of it without concerning
ourselves with causes. We should immediately propose
legislation to ban all ice cream sales.

Some advocates claim that it is the huge amounts of data that are
often associated with Big Data that eliminate the need for understanding causes. This claim is ludicrous, of course, but it's seriously
made by some software vendors, consultants, and authors. Until we
understand what causes things to occur, we don't understand how
to influence them. When we spot a correlation, it's too soon to
celebrate. Our work has only begun.

Unit Bias

Michael weighs a great deal more than Shawn. You can tell
just be looking at the size of his waist.

This is the tendency to attribute causation to a single salient factor
rather than taking all significant factors into account. In the
example above, most of us tend to consider people's waist size to a
much greater degree than their heights when estimating their
weight. When comparing people's weights, we often mistake people
with large waists as heavier than those with smaller waists who are
significantly taller. Michael's girth might stand out as the more
salient feature, but his height contributes just as much to his
weight.

   This bias stems in part from our desire to simplify things when
faced with complexity. It's typical for conclusions to be based
entirely or mostly on a single variable merely because it's easier
than the more thorough data sensemaking that's necessary.

Outcome Bias

Since Cheryl became the Operations Manager, defects in the
manufacturing process have decreased. Cheryl is definitely a
good manager.

This is the tendency to evaluate performance based solely on the
outcome. If the outcome is good, performance is judged to have

caused that good outcome without further investigation. When outcomes are good or bad, we tend to avoid thorough assessments of performance altogether, which is a mistake. We must try to understand actual causes before we can give credit to someone or something for good outcomes or blame them for bad outcomes. Until we confirm the actual causes of outcomes, we cannot be confident in our ability to produce or prevent them.

These causal errors have much in common. We can avoid them all by thinking more critically about the nature of cause.

For a more comprehensive look at the minefield of cognitive biases and logical fallacies that undermine not just data sense-making but reasoning in general, I recommend that you read *Thinking, Fast and Slow* by Daniel Kahneman and *Logically Fallacious* by Bo Bennett.

Now that we've considered the importance of critical thinking, in the next chapter we'll consider the importance of scientific thinking to our data-sensemaking loom.

CHAPTER 3 – THINK SCIENTIFICALLY

Scientific thinking is simply thinking that follows the scientific method. However, the scientific method, and science more generally, are often misunderstood. The media, and even people in day-to-day conversation, tend to speak of science as if everyone understands it, but, as it turns out, this is a bad assumption. Most people only have a vague sense of science—what it does and how it works. Surprisingly, there aren't many resources that explain science in accessible ways. This is, in part, because most scientists are notoriously bad at communicating what they do to non-scientists. Clear communication to the general public wasn't the focus of their training. In this chapter, I'll attempt to bridge this gap by distilling the essence of scientific thinking into clear and simple (but not simplistic) terms. Applying scientific principles is essential, along with applying the critical thinking principles we learned in Chapter 2, to building a sound structure on which we can weave a fabric of understanding from data.

Science

Science is a particular way to study the world. The world, in this context, is everything that exists—atoms, stars, rocks, plants, animals (including people), thoughts, emotions, etc.—and the forces that affect those entities. Science strives to understand these entities and forces: what they are, how they behave, and why they behave as they do. Science strives to provide both *descriptions* (answers to *what* and *how* questions) and *explanations* (answers to *why* questions). The goal of science is to understand the world as it really is.

We observe the world directly through our senses or indirectly through the use of instruments (microscopes, telescopes, thermometers, etc.) that can either detect and measure what our senses cannot or can do so to a greater degree or with greater precision. Anything that can be observed is in the realm of science. Some argue that science is solely concerned with the *natural world*, and that, if supernatural entities and forces exist, including gods, ghosts, psychic powers, and miracles, they reside outside the realm of science. This is an arbitrary and unnecessary distinction, however, for anything that can be observed can and should be subjected to scientific inquiry.

Science consists of many specialized domains of study, which can be grouped in various ways. Perhaps the most common distinguishes the *natural sciences* from the *social sciences*. Domains of natural science, such as physics, astronomy, biology, and botany, are concerned with the material world. The natural sciences are further subdivided into the *physical sciences* (physics, astronomy, etc.) and the *life sciences* (biology, botany, etc.). Domains of social science, such as anthropology, psychology, and sociology, are concerned with human behavior.

So far, in this section, I've left something vital out of my description of science. Here's a more complete definition:

> Science is the study of the world to understand what it is and how it works *using the scientific method*.

Not every study of the world qualifies as science. The scientific method is what sets science apart and makes it uniquely effective. This leads to the obvious question, "What is the scientific method?"

The Scientific Method

The scientific method is a set of principles and practices that direct the work of science. At its most fundamental level, the scientific method consists of two components: 1) *observations*, which are the evidence on which scientific knowledge is based, and 2) *logic*, which governs the interpretation of those observations. Science is *empir-

ical, which is just another way of saying that it's based on observations.

> *Sooner or later, the validity of scientific claims is settled by referring to observations of phenomena...When faced with a claim that something is true, scientists respond by asking what evidence supports it.[1]*

There is also a third and less-often-acknowledged fundamental component of the scientific method: *presuppositions*. In science, a presupposition is a belief about the world that cannot be proved but must be assumed for science to proceed. The most basic of science's presuppositions are the beliefs that the world is 1) real (i.e., it's not merely an illusion), 2) orderly (i.e., it's consistently governed by laws), and 3) accessible to human intelligence (i.e., it's potentially comprehensible). The presuppositions of science are neither arbitrary nor unwarranted; they are essential. Apart from its presuppositions, the scientific method deals solely with matters that are falsifiable; everything is subject to the possibility of being disproven.

This approach to making sense of the world emerged through many centuries of trial and error, but *modern science* mostly took shape during the period known as the *Scientific Revolution*, roughly between the years 1550 and 1700. Modern science challenges the intuitive notions of how the world works that we naturally develop during childhood, which are often wrong. As Robert Pirsig said in *Zen and the Art of Motorcycle Maintenance*:

> *The real purpose of the scientific method is to make sure Nature hasn't misled you into thinking you know something you don't actually know.[2]*

It was only through the scientific method that we were able to move beyond intuitive notions such as "the world is flat" to begin the journey of discovery that led to our modern technological world.

At their most basic level, steps in the scientific method are simple. We observe the world, and when we notice something that we don't understand, we propose explanations and test them. Scientific investigation always begins by recognizing a gap or flaw in our understanding. According to Matt Ridley:

> *The fuel on which science runs is ignorance. Science is like a hungry furnace that must be fed logs from the forests of ignorance that surround us. In the process, the clearing that we call knowledge expands, but the more it expands, the longer its perimeter and the more ignorance comes into view...A true scientist is bored by knowledge; it is the assault on ignorance that motivates him—the mysteries that previous discoveries have revealed. The forest is more interesting than the clearing.[3]*

A great deal of preparation is required to do the work of science. Scientists prepare by learning 1) the scientific method in general, 2) the specific research methods of their particular domain (physics, biology, psychology, etc.), and 3) the established body of knowledge that already exists in their domain. Science doesn't start from scratch with each new scientist. It builds on the work that has already been done; otherwise, science would never progress.

When scientists notice gaps or flaws in their understanding, they search for explanations. More specifically, they propose *hypotheses* (i.e., tentative explanations). As I mentioned in the previous chapter, scientific reasoning is primarily abductive in nature: testing hypotheses in search of the explanations that best fit the evidence, ever open to new evidence and better explanations.

A hypothesis is simply a potential explanation for how something works or what causes it to happen. It's an educated guess at an answer to a scientific question. If we ask the question, "What causes an electric motor to increase in speed?", we might hypothesize that an increase in electric current would do the trick. Once a hypothesis is proposed, it must be tested. How it's tested depends on the nature of the phenomenon under investigation. The two primary approaches to testing a hypothesis involve 1) doing experiments or, when experiments cannot be done, 2) observing phenomena as they naturally occur.

Experiments are particularly useful because they allow us to carefully control conditions to significantly reduce the possibility of confusion, such as attributing effects to one cause when in fact something else entirely created them. Imagine that we want to determine and compare the effects of two different fertilizers— Fertilizer A and Fertilizer B—on the growth of tomato plants. In an experiment, we would attempt to control every factor that could possibly contribute to plant growth other than the fertilizers, such as variations in soil composition or the amount of water that the plants receive. To test the fertilizers' effects experimentally, we might include 150 tomato plants in our study, all of which are the same type, size, and age, and were produced from the same source of seeds. We could accurately test the effects of the two fertilizers by dividing the plants into three groups of 50 plants each: one group receiving Fertilizer A, another receiving Fertilizer B, and the last receiving no fertilizer whatsoever. The third group with no fertilizer functions as a *control group*, which establishes a baseline against which to compare the two other groups. In this case the control group would reveal the amount of plant growth that naturally occurs without any fertilizer, which we would subtract from growth that's associated with the fertilizers to determine their actual effects. We could make sure that all of the plants are placed in containers of the same type and size, containing the same soil. We could also place them in a greenhouse that allows us to control atmospheric conditions, such as the amount of light that the plants receive and consistent protection from pests. Finally, we could use a drip watering system to deliver precisely the same amount of water to each plant at the same times each day. Assuming that we've identified all of the factors that could contribute to plant growth, we have designed an experiment that controls all relevant factors so that fertilizer alone is allowed to vary.

Any factor that can exist in differing types or amounts is called a *variable*. In our plant experiment, fertilizer is a variable in that it could exist in various types. Plant growth is also a variable in that it could exist in various amounts. Scientific studies always involve at least two types of variables—*independent* and *dependent*—and often involve *controlled* variables as well. We control variables by holding them constant to make sure that, if they exercise any influence over the effects, they do so in a consistent manner.

A dependent variable is the one that exhibits the effects that our study is observing. In our plant study, growth is the dependent variable. An independent variable is the one that is varied to produce the effects that we're observing in the dependent variable. Effects in the dependent variable *depend on* the independent variable. Our plant experiment is designed to test three conditions of our independent variable, which is fertilizer type: Fertilizer A, Fertilizer B, and no fertilizer.

As Stephen S. Carey explains:

> *The goal of a decisive test is to arrange circumstances under which we can be confident that nothing unforeseen or extraneous can invalidate the experiment's outcome. There are two potential sources of error that can affect an experiment's finding. A well planned experiment will be designed to avoid both.*
>
> *First, an experiment may overlook factors that can lead to false confirmation of the claim at issue…The way to minimize the possibility of a false confirmation is to set up experimental conditions that control for extraneous factors— factors other than the claim at issue that might lead to the predicted result…A second source of experimental error involves overlooking factors which can lead to a false rejection of the claim being tested…So, of any experimental test, we need to ask a second question: has anything been overlooked that might lead to a failure to get the predicted outcome even if the claim at issue is right?*[4]

It's possible for a scientific study to have more than one independent variable, but studies of this type are complex; they must consider the effects on the dependent variable of all possible combinations of the independent variables. Each combination becomes a separate condition in the study. For example, imagine a study that considers the effects of both sleep deprivation and time of day on the occurrence of driving accidents.

It's also possible for a study to have more than one dependent variable. For example, imagine a study of the effects of fertilizers to determine both 1) increases in plant size and 2) increases in the number of tomatoes that each plant bears.

Unfortunately, not everything that we care about in science can be tested experimentally. In some situations, we must rely on *observational studies*. For example, if we hypothesize that a diet rich in refined sugar contributes to childhood obesity, it wouldn't be ethical to feed kids a diet that might be harmful. In such a case, the best we could do is observe children who, due to no influence from us, have diets rich in refined sugar, and compare their rates of obesity to similar kids who don't have diets rich in refined sugar. Obviously, observational studies might not be as controlled as well-designed experimental studies. They're still useful, just less certain.

Clearly, hypotheses are central to the scientific method. Given their importance, you might assume that scientists diligently strive only to confirm their hypotheses, but this isn't the case. When scientists follow the scientific method, they strive even more diligently to *dis*confirm their hypotheses—to prove that they aren't true. Because we naturally want our notions to be true, we're tempted to look only for evidence that confirms them. *Confirmation bias*, which we touched on previously, lies at the root of many false conclusions. Scientists strive to overcome confirmation bias by doing their best to disprove their hypotheses. If a hypothesis withstands their fervent efforts to disprove it, resulting in no disconfirming evidence and only confirming evidence, then and only then can scientists legitimately claim that the hypothesis might be true.

According to Randall K. Noon, a good working hypothesis exhibits the following characteristics:

- *All the data upon which it is based needs to be factually verifiable.*
- *It must be consistent with all the relevant verifiable data, not just selected data.*
- *The scientific principles upon which the hypothesis relies must be verifiable and repeatable.*

- *The hypothesis should provide some predictive value.*
- *The hypothesis must be subjected to and withstand genuine falsifiable efforts.*[5]

Scientists work hard to propose good hypotheses, but don't consider it a failure when their hypotheses fail to withstand scrutiny. Even when the explanatory power of a hypothesis is rejected, scientists can still learn something that gets them closer to understanding.

Whether scientists test a hypothesis using an experimental or observational study, they collect data, interpret it, and eventually publish their findings. They do so transparently by clearly and thoroughly describing what they did and by making their data available for others to examine. The larger scientific community then gets involved by reviewing the study to confirm that the conclusions are valid. This is done not only by reviewing published studies but also by retesting hypotheses in subsequent studies, either by carrying out careful *replications* of the original study or by designing different studies altogether. The process of reviewing studies and retesting hypotheses is an essential part of the scientific method.

Something happens when a hypothesis is tested over and over and consistently survives scrutiny. It becomes a *theory*. Contrary to this term's use in everyday conversation, in science a theory is an explanation that has earned confidence. Biological evolution was once a hypothesis but is now a theory. Similarly, the germ theory of disease began as a hypothesis. In addition to a higher level of confidence, scientific theories also tend to be explanations that are broader in scope than hypotheses.

> *What typifies theories in science is the breadth and depth of their explanatory power. A hypothesis typically will offer an explanation for a limited range of phenomena, a single event, or a fact. Theories tend to be more general structures capable of explaining a much wider variety of phenomena. Moreover, theories will often contain well-confirmed rules and principles that reveal underlying explanatory similarities between apparently quite diverse phenomena.*[6]

Objectivity is another important characteristic of the scientific method. Science strives to eliminate biases and perceptual distortions. It attempts to remain independent from cultural and individual perspectives. Whether scientific work is done in the United States, Germany, China, or Slovenia, the results should be the same. Whether it's done by Cheryl, Charlie, George, or Sally, it should adhere to the same principles and practices. Is absolute objectivity possible? Absolutely not, but the scientific method gets us closer to that ideal. The goal is "observer-independent truths about a world independent of us" that are "public and verifiable" and immune to worldview differences.[7]

Finally, the scientific method emphasizes the *tentativeness* of its findings. Science produces highly probable results that are always subject to revisions, not truths that are certain and never-changing. One of the essential tenets of science is its perpetual openness to correction. The fact that scientific understanding changes in response to new findings is a strength, not a weakness. Certainty is not a trustworthy path to understanding. The scientific method encourages *self-correction*.

In summary, the scientific method is:

- *Based on presuppositions* that the world is real, orderly, and accessible to human intelligence
- *Empirical*
- *Logical*
- *Objective*
- *Falsifiable*
- *Controlled*
- *Focused on disconfirmation*
- *Transparent*
- *Confirmed through multiple tests*
- *Probable*
- *Tentative* and *self-correcting*

For a more thorough yet still accessible description of the scientific method, I recommend Stephen S. Carey's excellent book, *A Beginner's Guide to Scientific Method*.

Science is the best means that we've developed to make sense of the world, step by halting step. To science, we owe the development of many life-enhancing technologies. The better we understand the world, the better off we'll be. It should come as no surprise, then, that the understanding we develop through data sensemaking can be deeply enriched by applying the scientific method.

Applying the Scientific Method to Data Sensemaking

How much of the scientific method should we apply to data sensemaking? As much as possible. How often should we apply it? As often as possible and practical. We can and should conduct much of our work scientifically, adopting a scientific mindset. Even if our organization does not operate in a scientific domain—most don't—what we do nevertheless belongs to a domain to which we can apply the scientific method. We should think of our data-sensemaking projects as research studies. Similar to scientists, we look for gaps and flaws in our understanding and conduct studies to address them. The border that exists between uses of the scientific method by scientists in a research lab versus data sensemakers in a company's analytics group is often fairly arbitrary.

Although it's true that the scientific method is rarely followed by data sensemakers, except in minor ways, it should be. Circumstances will not always allow us to fully apply the scientific method, but we should keep in mind that, in those cases, our findings will be less reliable. The aim of developing reliable findings motivates us to employ the scientific method whenever and to the greatest degree possible.

Let's consider nine specific aspects of the scientific method that we can and should often apply to our work as data sensemakers.

1. Propose and test hypotheses

We construct hypotheses informally whenever we ask questions and then look to data for answers. These hypotheses can initially be based on simple intuitions. When asking the question, "What is causing customers to abandon our service?" we might propose any one of the following hypotheses:

> "Customers are abandoning our service because they are unhappy with our rates."

> "Customers are abandoning our service because they think our competitors offer a better service."

> "Customers are abandoning our service because they no longer need it."

Transforming this informal process of asking questions into one that involves hypotheses more formally can produce more trustworthy findings. We should write our hypotheses down, weigh their relative merits based on what we already know, and then test those that seem most likely. We should subject them to scrutiny by digging into the data. If, at any point, the data shows that our hypothesis is false, we should record our findings and move on to the next candidate.

I'm suggesting that we make the proposal and testing of hypotheses a more conscious and methodical process. Otherwise, we tend to ask and answer questions too casually, often missing important clues. Formalizing the process encourages us to follow through, even when hypotheses are difficult to test. When the process is casual, it's too easy to only pursue questions that are easy to answer and ignore the others. Formalizing the process also creates accountability, even if only to ourselves.

2. Conduct experiments

The data that is already available to us is not always adequate. In such cases, we either need to find additional data that supplies what's lacking, if that data exists, or run an experiment to produce additional data. Many data sensemakers limit the scope of their work to existing data. This is unfortunate and arbitrary. When existing data is lacking, we can sometimes conduct experiments to generate exactly what's needed. Experiments aren't always an option, but when they are, they can usually provide a surer path to understanding.

Imagine that we work for a company that identifies products that customers might want based on purchasing or browsing behavior and then recommends those products to customers via email. In other words, we have a recommendation system, similar to those that are found on popular consumer sites such as Amazon.com or entertainment sites such as Netflix. Now imagine that we ask the question, "To what extent are customers purchasing the products that we recommend to them?" We might hypothesize that customers purchase the products that we recommend at least 25% of the time. At this point, we could use the data that's already available to identify all of the recommendations that were made during a particular period of time (e.g., a particular month) and then check to see whether the products that were recommended were subsequently purchased by customers within a particular period of time (e.g., within 30 days after the recommendation was made) at least 25% of the time. What this wouldn't tell us, however, is the extent to which those customers would have purchased those products even if we hadn't recommended them. Knowing this would be useful as well.

As an experiment, we could identify a particular product and, for a specified period of time, send emails to recommend it only to every other customer whose behavior indicates potential interest. Doing this would divide the full population of customers who are identified as having a potential interest in the product into two randomly selected groups: Group 1 would receive an email recommending the product, and Group 2 would serve as the control group, receiving no such email. Having collected the data, we could compare the number of times that customers in Group 1 purchased the product to the number of times that customers in Group 2 did so and then subtract the number of Group 2 purchases from Group 1 purchases to come up with a number that could legitimately be attributed to the recommendation. If that number represents a 25% or greater rate of purchase, thus confirming our hypothesis, we could go on to replicate this same test several more times with

other products. In so doing, we might find that our recommendations always produce a success rate within a particular range, such
as from 30% to 40%. On the other hand, we might find that the
success rate varies significantly depending on the product that's
recommended, which would lead us to propose new hypotheses
that could be explored through additional, more fine-tuned
experiments.

It takes time to design and conduct experiments. It's often worth
it, however, when the effort could produce more reliable findings.

3. Use representative data

We can improve the quality of data sensemaking by making sure
that our data represents the relevant population well. A *population*,
in this context, is a group that includes every one of its members.
The population of U.S. residents includes everyone who resides in
the U.S., not just U.S. citizens. The population of a company's sales
during a specified period of time includes every single sales transaction that occurred during that period. Whenever we use data to
answer questions, those questions are relevant to a particular
population.

To make sure that a data set represents the relevant population
well, we must first identify that population clearly. What boundaries define the population that we're trying to understand? If we're
trying to make sense of customer behavior, are we interested in all
or some subset of our customers? If all, we must also decide if we're
interested in current customers as of a particular date, a broader
swath of history, or customers at some point in the past. If a subset,
we must delineate this clearly as well. For example, we might decide
that we're only concerned with customers that represent a particular industry (e.g., health care providers), those of a particular size,
or those in a particular geographical area. When we define a
population and then isolate data that represents that population
only, we do so with the clear understanding that our findings will
only apply to that population. We can't study health care providers
only and assume that their behavior characterizes other customers
as well.

The more narrowly we define the population, the more easily we'll usually be able to generate or collect data about it. This is fine if our interest is legitimately narrow, but it's a problem if we want to acquire knowledge that has broader application. Obviously, general knowledge is more often useful than knowledge about a limited group. Learning something that's true of all our customers is more often useful than learning something that is only true of a few customers. General knowledge usually takes more time and effort to develop, however.

Once we've defined our population, we might include data for every single member or, when that's impossible or impractical, a representative sample. A *sample* is a subset of a population. A *representative sample* is one that does an adequate job of reflecting the population as a whole in all its variety.

To guarantee that a sample represents the whole, we must include enough members to capture the population's variety. By selecting the members that are included in the sample randomly (i.e., by chance), we can be fairly confident that the variation of the sample is similar in type and proportion to that of the population as a whole. The size needed for an effective sample depends, in part, on the variation within the population. If members of a population are alike in most respects, with little variation, a fairly small sample, perhaps as few as 20, could be adequate. If, however, members differ in several ways (i.e., related to many variables) and to a significant degree, samples must be much larger to represent that variation. This is why proper polls that predict voter behavior must consider people who vary significantly, and in many ways (location, education, income, age, race, etc.). Well-designed polls that predict voter behavior in the U.S. as a whole sample thousands of people and select them randomly.

In most scientific domains, data sets that represent entire populations are rarely feasible. This is especially true in experimental studies. In some scientific domains, and fairly often in the data sensemaking that we do in many organizations (e.g., businesses), we can include data for an entire population because it's readily available. In these cases, unless there's a good reason why the entire data set can't be included, such as a data set that is too large to process with available technologies, it makes sense to include it all.

4. Control the variables

It can be difficult at times to control factors other than our independent variables, which alone should vary. Factors that can affect the dependent variable, other than the independent variable, are called *confounders, confounding factors,* or *confounding variables.* Something confounds if it can be mistaken for something else. Historical attempts to draw conclusions about race as an independent variable were often confounded by other factors, such as wealth and education level. We can control confounding variables by holding them constant—that is, by not allowing them to vary—while still allowing the independent variable to vary. In our imagined fertilizer experiment described earlier, we controlled soil conditions by making sure that all containers were filled with soil from the exact same source.

Imagine that we want to determine the best place to position a particular chart on a computer screen to make sure that those who view the screen see it first, before anything else. If we simply hook people up to eye-trackers and show them a bunch of screens that display charts and observe where they look, this would not control the many factors besides position on the screen (size, color, brightness, type of chart, etc.) that could determine what catches people's eyes when the screen initially appears. This would be a poorly controlled experiment, with results that would be inconclusive. Indeed, it would qualify as pseudoscience. Instead, we could design an experiment that varied nothing but the position of the chart. For example, we could design a screen that contained several charts that are consistent in type, size, color, etc., and then use eye-tracking software to determine where people look first. In addition, we might also use a blank screen—one that includes no content whatsoever—to see where people look first when there is nothing in particular to see. In other words, blank screens could function as a control group.

Similarly, in observational studies, even though we can't design conditions to be controlled, we can narrow the data set to include only members that exhibit a particular expression of each confounding variable. For example, if we're trying to understand the effects of a particular marketing campaign on customer purchases, and we suspect that customer size might be a confounding factor, we could test our hypothesis on a data set that only includes customers of a particular size, such as large customers.

The downside of controlling variables in this manner, as you perhaps suspect, is that we can't assume that our findings will apply to all expressions of those factors. If we narrowed the data set to include only large customers in the study mentioned previously, it would remain possible that customers of other sizes might exhibit significantly different purchasing behavior. To apply our findings more generally, we could make separate observations for each of its variations. For example, we could study the effects of our marketing campaigns on purchasing behavior separately for small customers, medium-sized customers, and large customers. To do this, we don't necessarily need to make our observations in a series of independent tests. Instead, we could do it all at once by segregating the data into subsets—one for each expression of the confounding factor—and then examining the results of each subset separately. If our hypothesis is confirmed in all cases, we would have reason to believe that our results were not influenced by the confounding factors.

5. Attempt to disconfirm hypotheses

We should always attempt to disconfirm our hypotheses as much as we attempt to confirm them. It's tempting to look for confirmation only and to do so quickly, before any contradictory evidence might show up, but our results wouldn't be trustworthy. It takes more time to seek disconfirmation, but it produces more reliable results. Seeking only to confirm our hypotheses rather than to both disconfirm and confirm them might seem like a small difference, but the effect is huge. By doing this routinely, we can combat confirmation bias, and in so doing, open our eyes to unexpected and perhaps inconvenient findings.

6. Search for causes

Understanding causal relationships gives us potential control over outcomes. But not all knowledge is equal in value. Understanding what causes heath to improve, profits to increase, or manufacturing defects to decrease is more useful than merely knowing that people, profits, or defects do better in the west region than elsewhere. Why do they do better? If we understand why, we can use that knowledge to encourage the beneficial results that we desire.

Too often, data sensemaking focuses solely on collecting and reporting facts. However, facts are only useful if they lead to an understanding that enables decisions and actions that produce a better world. Not every important question involves causal relationships, but the most important questions usually do.

7. Test the predictive power of findings

Understanding what has happened in the past is interesting, but it isn't terribly useful if it tells us nothing about the future. When we understand causes—why things behave as they do—we can use that understanding to predict what will happen in the future. Before we start relying on any particular understanding, however, we should first examine its predictive power. When we do, we will at times learn that our findings were circumstantial and therefore not at all predictive in the way that we hoped. When a hypothesis holds up to scrutiny, even after we diligently attempt to disconfirm it, we're not done. We should go on to use our findings to predict what will happen in a new situation and then collect new data to test that prediction. With each successful prediction, our findings will become more reliable and useful.

8. Publish the findings

Documenting and publishing our data-sensemaking findings, much as scientists document their research studies, serves many purposes. Here are a few:

- It provides a personal record—a written memory—that we can refer to in the future.
- It provides an organizational record that others can access and learn from.
- It contributes to a foundation of knowledge that can be built on in the future.
- It supplies source material for collaboration.
- It encourages us to think clearly, thoroughly, and carefully about our work as we're doing it.
- It functions as a checklist of sorts to keep us from omitting vital steps.
- It provides those who rely on our work with thorough answers to their questions, thus promoting their understanding.
- It can increase awareness of our work and its value throughout the organization.

We should document our studies in a way that can be understood by anyone who might benefit from our findings, not just by our immediate peers. Also, we should document our studies regardless of our findings. A study that disconfirms a hypothesis provides useful information.

Our research reports should include the following:

- Statement of purpose (i.e., why we did the work, including what we were hoping to achieve)
- Hypotheses that we tested
- Research design, including descriptions of the steps we took, the data we examined, and the statistics we applied
- Conclusions and our thoughts about them
- Evidence on which our conclusions were based
- Any assumptions on which our conclusions were based
- Everything useful that we learned in addition to our conclusions
- Flaws and/or limitations of the work
- Suggested future work
- A means to access the data that we examined so that others can review or use it

This is what scientists include in well-written research papers. When we take enough time to clearly and thoroughly document our work in this manner, we contribute substantially to the storehouse of knowledge. When these reports are stored electronically in a consistent manner that is searchable throughout the organization and perhaps beyond, the value of our work is magnified. Unfortunately, in my experience, I've found that most of the work done by data sensemakers is stored nowhere except in their flawed memories and perhaps a few disorganized records. This is a terrible waste of important information.

9. Collaborate.

When we document our work properly, we enable the possibility of collaboration. Peer reviews and replication of our work by others are two powerful forms of collaboration that are encouraged in scientific communities. Just as scientists have peers, we who work as data sensemakers in organizations of all types usually have peers as well. We can learn a great deal by allowing them to review our work. Peer reviews, done properly, accomplish more than the mere correction of errors. They also allow us to learn from one another when we suggest improvements.

A great deal of informal collaboration other than peer reviews is possible if we share what we're doing with others. Collaboration is especially useful when we need fresh input or perspectives. For example, when trying to answer a particular question with data, we might, after creating a list of potential hypotheses, describe the situation to colleagues and ask them to review our list and propose additional hypotheses to consider. They might also point out existing evidence that disconfirms one or more of our hypotheses.

Another possibility, still in its infancy, is that of shared best practices. In science, much of the work in any domain is guided by paradigms—shared ways of thinking about the topic, and how to handle it. Such paradigms enable scientists to avoid reinventing the wheel, allowing their efforts to focus on new challenges. The sharing of knowledge about approaches and ways of thinking about particular kinds of problems in sensemaking may offer similarly great benefits.

None of us can do our work as well in a vacuum as we can when collaborating with other skilled data sensemakers. Also, data sensemakers who are still in the early stages of developing their skills will needlessly flounder if they work in isolation. Even if you're a loner, as I tend to be, you need to find companions. Talking to ourselves can only take us so far.

―――――――――――――――――――――

In the remaining chapters, the topics that we'll address are founded on both scientific thinking and critical thinking, which together form a sturdy loom on which to weave understanding from data.

CHAPTER 4 – QUESTION THE DATA

Data sensemaking, from start to finish, involves asking questions of data in pursuit of accurate, meaningful, and useful answers. It's important that we ask the right questions.

> *It is not possible to become a good thinker and be a poor questioner. Thinking is not driven by answers but, rather, by questions.*[1]

Before we ask questions *of* the data, however, we must ask a number of critical questions *about* the data.

Let's begin by thinking a bit about the nature of data. Data sets are composed of individual data fields. Data fields are either *categorical* or *quantitative* in nature. Categorical fields, usually expressed as words, describe the categories to which things belong. For example, if we're trying to understand how our products are selling, we might examine the following categories:

- Product Name
- Product Version
- Customer Name
- Customer Location
- Customer Type
- Order Date

Categorical fields contain one or more items. For example, the category *Customer Type* might consist of the following items: *business, government, health care, education,* and *non-profit* customers. Categorical fields describe what things are. We understand our world, in part, by assigning things to categories and giving them names.

Quantitative fields, expressed as numbers, count or measure things, such as the following sales-related fields:

- Revenue
- Unit Price
- Items Sold
- Discount Percentage

Quantitative fields describe *how many* things there are or *how much* there is of something. We always associate quantitative data with categorical data. Numbers that aren't associated with something are meaningless. Both categorical and quantitative data function as *variables*; instances of them can vary within some set of items (categorical) or range of values (quantitative).

Now we're ready to consider the questions that we should ask about the data. These questions address the following topics:

- Required data
- Relevance of the data
- Semantics of the data
- Source of the data
- Accuracy of the data
- Completeness of the data
- Context of the data
- Representativeness of the data
- Causes of the behaviors recorded in the data
- Aggregation of the data
- Expression of the data

Required Data

The question: "What data is required for the task at hand?"

In general, data sensemaking falls into two broad types: exploratory and directed. *Exploratory data sensemaking* (a.k.a., exploratory data analysis or EDA) does not begin with a specific question but instead entails exploring data freely to get the lay of the land, to become familiar with it overall. We look for anything that is informative and potentially useful. This open-ended exploration allows us to develop a broad understanding that gives context to any specific questions that we subsequently ask of the data. Exploratory data sensemaking is valuable in part because it gives us an opportunity to be surprised by information that we never knew to look for or ask about. Some of the greatest treasures that reside in data are unanticipated.

In contrast, *directed data sensemaking* begins with one or more specific questions and then looks for answers. It has a particular purpose. During the course of any organization's work, specific issues arise that need answers. Much data sensemaking is driven by these issues and is therefore directed in nature.

When we look for answers to specific questions, it's important to determine, before we proceed, what fields of data are required to answer those questions. This is the same concern that scientists deal with when they strive to understand something. According to Stephen S. Carey, when scientists make observations, they must ask the following two questions:

1. *Do we have a clear sense of what the relevant phenomena are?*
2. *Have we found a way to insure we have not overlooked anything in the process of making our observations?*[2]

Any data set that we examine will powerfully influence and potentially limit our ability to answer the questions that we ask of it. Stated differently, the data set will frame our perceptions. It will lead us in a particular direction and potentially restrict what we find. Answers that are based on incomplete data sets are unreliable.

We sometimes ask the same questions of data repeatedly over time because we need to understand whether things have changed, whether the answer now differs from the answer in the past. When we query data over and over, it's tempting to automatically examine the same data fields that we examined to answer the same question in the past. We should occasionally resist this temptation. It's possible that we didn't examine all of the right data in the past, leading to inadequate or even incorrect answers. We can go merrily on our way asking the same question and getting the same answer each time—possibly the same wrong answer. We should bring fresh eyes to the task. If we do, we might think of other, more useful, data to consider.

We must take time to think deeply about the questions that we're asking so that we can determine in advance, as well as possible, which data fields and which instances of those fields are needed to answer our questions. Instances could range from all of the data that's available to some subset of records, such as a limited group or a particular period of time. Once we begin the data-sensemaking process, we will occasionally realize that other data fields or records are needed beyond those that we anticipated, but this doesn't diminish the benefits of doing our best to imagine what's needed in advance. We can create a list of the data fields that are needed and for each determine the set of records that are needed. With this in hand, we can then acquire the data that's needed.

In the real world, we will at times discover that the ideal data set isn't available. In these cases, we will need to determine whether the limited data that's available will lend itself to answers that are good enough, keeping in mind that those limitations will reduce the reliability of our findings.

All of the remaining questions about the data that we'll consider in this chapter will assume that a data set has already been selected or provided.

Relevance of the Data

The question: "Are all of these data fields relevant to the task at hand?"

I've seen people report outlandish findings—weave highly imaginative and completely erroneous stories—because they assumed that every field of data that they were provided to answer a particular question was relevant to the task. The data visualization competition that I described in Chapter 1 provided many examples of this.

In that competition, you may recall that participants were assigned the following task: "Based on the data set that has been provided, identify the best sales opportunities for our company's devices for treating strokes." To perform this task, they were provided the following data fields:

- Hospital (ID and name)
- Hospital location (latitude and longitude, city, state, and whether urban or rural)
- Total stroke admissions to the hospital (including readmissions) for the year 2015
- Total stroke admissions to the hospital (including readmissions) for the year 2016
- Stroke readmission rate for the year 2016
- Average length of hospital stay in days for stroke admission for the year 2016

Had the participants thought critically about the task before diving into the data, they would have realized that sales opportunities consisted of hospitals with patients who were suffering from strokes that their company's devices could treat, but only hospitals that hadn't already purchased an adequate supply of those products.

No one seemed to notice that several of the data fields were irrelevant to the task. Whether a hospital was urban or rural would only be relevant as a way to determine the cost of sales if rural hospitals required more effort because their location was far from urban centers where the sales staff would likely be based. Readmission rates would only potentially be relevant if we knew the reasons why patients were readmitted. It's possible that few readmissions would provide new opportunities for stroke treatment devices. Variation in lengths of stay can be caused by several factors, including patient death, patient improvement, differences in the quality of care, and even the part of the brain that's affected by the stroke, which could cause different conditions that might require different treatment periods. Without knowing this context, the length of stay cannot help us identify sales opportunities. Also, the average length of stay expressed as the mean is not an appropriate measure of central tendency because its variation is highly skewed as we discussed earlier. Means should only be used as measures of central tendency for sets of values that are distributed from lowest to highest in a bell-shaped manner, called *normal distributions*. Two consecutive years of annual stroke admission counts are not adequate for determining a trend or anticipating future demand. Only admission counts were relevant to the assigned task, but they were inadequate in and of themselves.

Despite the irrelevance of several data fields, competitors proceeded to base all sorts of conclusions on them. As you might imagine, those conclusions conflicted with one another. Because the competitors didn't begin by thinking critically about the task, they allowed the data that was provided to frame their answers, assuming that all of the data fields must have been relevant and complete. That was a mistake.

We can't trust that a data set—one that's been provided by someone else rather than carefully pieced together by us—is entirely relevant. It's up to us to identify and disregard all that isn't relevant. If people provide us with data that seems irrelevant, we should question them about it. It's always possible that we're missing something. If, on the other hand, they're mistaken in providing data that's not relevant to the task, we've done them and ourselves a favor by asking the question.

Semantics of the Data

The question: "What do the various fields of data mean?"

Whenever we examine a particular data set to make sense of it, we must understand the semantics of the data—what each data field means. We can't assume the meaning, and we certainly shouldn't guess because meaning often isn't obvious. We must find out.

These are not mere matters of semantics. There is nothing *mere* about semantics. The meanings of things are essential to understanding, and shared meanings are essential to communication.

Consider the seemingly straightforward term *revenue*. What exactly qualifies as revenue? The term can be defined in many ways. If we encounter a data field called revenue in a data set, we must find out what revenue means in that particular context. This is sometimes fairly easy because a data dictionary has been developed to document agreements about the meanings of variables. Even when this is the case, however, there is still a risk that the people who created the data set or those who wish to use it are not aware of or do not agree with the data dictionary. For this reason, it's wise to confirm definitions.

To illustrate this concern, I'll use an example once again from the data visualization competition that we have been discussing. One of the fields in the data set that was provided for competitors was labeled *2016 Total Stroke Admissions*. A companion document that competitors were provided helpfully pointed out that this variable was a count of people who were admitted to the hospital in the year 2016 for stroke treatment, including readmissions. Knowing that readmissions were included was a vital piece of information. Other vital pieces of information were missing, however. One of the first questions that came to my mind when I reviewed the data set was, "If someone was admitted to the hospital for stroke treatment in December of 2015 and then readmitted for further treatment in January of 2016, was the 2016 readmission counted in 2015, in 2016, or in both?" (In addition, I wanted to understand why a separate count of readmissions was not also included in the data set so competitors could determine the number of people who were treated for strokes independent from the number of times they were admitted to the hospital, but this concern is separate from our present focus on semantics).

To make sense of data, we must clearly understand the meaning of each variable. If clear meaning has not been provided, we should seek it before proceeding.

Source of the Data

The question: "What is the source of the data and is it credible?"

It's important to know the source of the data that we're examining: what individuals, groups, systems, or processes produced it? This is important, in part, because the source might not be reliable. Some people, systems, or processes cannot be trusted. For example, some people have agendas. Some might even intentionally lie. Some simply lack the skill that's required to produce reliable data. Before taking time to examine data, we should confirm that it's from a trustworthy source. Even though sources lacking credibility can produce data that's reliable, we must evaluate data from such sources very diligently. Better yet, if they're available, we can turn to other sources that are more reliable.

We must keep in mind that the source of the data is not necessarily the person, group, or system from which we acquired it. We're concerned with the original source. Data sets get passed around all the time, often by people who have no clue whether the source is credible. We must trace the data set back to its origins. In their book *What the Numbers Say*, Derrick Niederman and David Boyum, speaking about the origins of quantitative data, argue:

> *The story behind a number is often as interesting and important as the number itself. That story is ignored at our peril, because the many steps involved in creating a number affect what information is captured in that number and how that number is likely to be interpreted and used. So if we really want to understand a number, we must take a hard look at how it was created.*[3]

Every data set that's produced for use by others should be documented so that its pedigree can be easily traced. Should be, but often isn't. If this information isn't available, we can't assume that all is well. In fact, if this information is missing, our suspicions should be aroused.

Even official data sources, such as corporate data warehouses, include erroneous data, which creeps in for various reasons. One common source of error is the substitution of zero for a missing value. If the number of students who enrolled in a particular class is missing for some reason, perhaps due to a clerical error, that does not mean that zero students enrolled in the class. It would be a mistake to declare the class a failure or to cancel its funding because of a clerical error, but judgments and actions like this sometimes occur.

I mentioned the importance of knowing a data set's pedigree above. This includes the entire chain of modifications that have been made to the data from its origins to its current state. This information should always accompany a data set, updated whenever changes are made. If we can't entirely trace the data set's pedigree, we can't trust it.

Accuracy of the Data

The question: "Is the data accurate?"

Asking if the data is accurate is different from asking if its source is credible. Credible sources can make errors, and unreliable sources can produce data that is accurate, despite reasonable suspicions to the contrary. How we determine the accuracy of data varies depending on the circumstances. Sometimes the data is well governed by quality controls that we've already learned to trust. When this isn't the case, it's useful to compare the data that's provided with data in the original source systems. For example, imagine a sales data mart that is composed of data from a sales transaction system. In such a case, we could extract data from that sales system and compare it to extracts from the data mart to confirm that they're consistent. If we find that they're not, it doesn't necessarily mean that the data mart is inaccurate. It could mean that our extract from the original source failed to account for business rules that were legitimately applied to alter the data after it was extracted from the sales system. In such cases, we can learn something valuable in the process of confirming the data's accuracy.

There is a tendency today, especially among advocates of Big Data, to minimize the importance of data accuracy. They argue that huge volumes of data overcome any concerns that we might have about data quality. In other words, when you have so much data, how could errors make much of a difference? Don't buy this argument. Errors in data tend to accumulate as a rate of error, not an absolute number. While it's true that 10 errors in a data set that consists of only 100 records should concern us more than 10 errors in a data set of 1,000,000 records, it's not true that an error rate of 10% in a data set of 1,000,000 records should concern us less than a

10% error rate in a data set of 100 records. Only a tiny rate of error can be ignored without peril.

This isn't the place to deal comprehensively with the methods to confirm the accuracy of data. What's important for our present purposes is to remember that data is sometimes inaccurate and that inaccuracy produces misunderstanding, so the question of accuracy must be considered.

Completeness of the Data

The question: "Does the data set include all that's needed?

Recall that the first question we asked was, "What data is required for the task at hand?" If we've answered that question, it's easy to determine whether a particular data set that's been provided includes everything that we need. If it doesn't, we either need to acquire what's missing or decide that our findings will be limited due to "known unknowns" and keep this in mind when making decisions or informing others. Unfortunately, it's much easier to construct stories when we lack information. The less we know, the easier it is to fit the pieces into the coherent story, for there are few facts to reconcile. We don't need good stories, however; we need the truth, and truth doesn't come easily. Understanding isn't complete if it's based on incomplete data.

Never accept a data set as complete without first thinking deeply about the data that's needed to do the job, regardless of the data that was provided. In the data visualization competition that I mentioned earlier, the fellow who organized the competition assumed that the data set was complete because it was provided by someone in the Marketing Department. Surely a marketing professional would know what data was needed to answer the question, "What are the best sales opportunities for our company's stroke treatment devices?" He should, but in this case he goofed. We can't always assume that others have done their jobs properly.

Context of the Data

The question: "Have I taken all of the relevant context into account?"

We can have all of the facts that directly address a particular question but fail utterly in understanding them if we don't consider their context. Nothing can be properly understood independent of its context. For example, in noticing that a particular country is not selling a particular product, you might conclude that it's unpopular in that country if you don't understand that the laws of that country restrict its sales. Facts can take on entirely different meanings in different contexts.

Some of the context that we must understand can be learned through exploratory data sensemaking. Broad familiarity with the data provides the context in which individual facts can be understood. Sufficient context doesn't always reside within data sets, however. Context is also learned from other sources, such as by reading an organization's publications, doing the actual work of the organization, or sometimes even by having conversations around the water cooler.

Focusing in on the details without context can result in myopia. Whereas *analysis* focuses on the details—breaking things down into their component parts and examining each individually—*synthesis* does the opposite. Synthesis involves stepping back to see the bigger picture—how the parts interact with one another to form a whole. There is an entire field of study called *systems science* or *systems thinking* that seeks to understand things in context, as dynamic systems rather than parts. Understanding requires both synthesis and analysis, the yin and yang of data sensemaking.

Representativeness of the Data

The Question: "Is what's revealed in the data typical?"

In addition to finding what the data reveals, we should determine if it's typical. We can determine whether behavior that we observe in data is routine or random by examining it in historical context. Doing so allows us to establish the range within which values routinely vary. This requires a reasonable amount of historical information consisting of several intervals of time. For example, if we have monthly values (i.e., as opposed the smaller periods, such as daily values), we would usually need more than a year's worth (i.e., more than 12 monthly values) to determine the routine range within which those values vary. If values fall within the range that's routine, we still care about them, but we don't need to react to them as a harbinger of something novel.

If the behavior that we observe in data is unusual, determining its cause is an important next step. It's possible that the behavior is entirely random—not due to a discernible cause. When this is the case, it makes no sense to be concerned, and it certainly makes no sense to respond because random events, by definition, cannot be controlled. People have on occasion lost their jobs because some performance metric looked bad entirely due to randomness. As data sensemakers, we should do our best to prevent this from happening.

When unusual behavior isn't random, discovering its cause creates potential opportunities for control. For example, if we know that particular defects in a manufacturing process are caused by malfunctions in a particular machine, we can fix or replace that machine. Understanding the nature of cause is our next topic.

Causes of the Behaviors Recorded in the Data

The Question: "What is causing this to happen?"

Under the banner of Big Data, some advocates have claimed that we no longer need to be concerned with causation. Spotting a correlation between two or more variables is supposedly enough; they assert that we can take advantage of that correlation without understanding it. I hope you recognize the absurdity of this claim. We can certainly take actions in response to correlations without understanding them, but doing so is risky. Unless we understand actual causes, we can't predict the ramifications of our actions.

Uncovering what causes things to happen is an essential pursuit of science. Even when causes seem obvious, our understanding is unreliable until we've put it to the test.

Aggregation of the Data

The Question: "Is the level at which the data has been aggregated and the statistical method that was used to produce that aggregation appropriate for the task at hand?"

When we examine data, we rarely do so at the finest level of detail. We usually aggregate the data to some degree. For example, when we examine sales data, for most purposes we don't look at each sales transaction individually (e.g., on September 9, 2018 the customer named Big Box Store purchased 10 of our televisions for $199.99 each). A detailed level of transactional information is sometimes useful, but not for most data-sensemaking tasks. When examining sales, we might, for most purposes, sum sales transactions for a particular product per day, week, or month. For other purposes, we might aggregate the data to that same level based on the mean rather than the sum. Different levels and methods of aggregation serve different purposes. For this reason, it usually makes sense to have access to the finest levels of detail in the data and then aggregate the data as needed in various ways.

When the data that's available has already been aggregated in a particular way, we should question the appropriateness of that aggregation. A good example can be found in the data visualization competition that we've been discussing. The number of days that patients who were treated at hospitals for strokes was aggregated based on the mean per hospital per year. We could argue that an annual aggregate wasn't detailed enough to understand how this value was changing through time. We could also argue that length of stay should have been aggregated based on the type of stroke that patients suffered and the part of the brain that was damaged because those factors strongly influence the time required for treatment and recovery. Perhaps even more important, we could argue that the mean was not an appropriate method of aggregation at all in this case. Why? Because the number of days that patients stay in the hospital when admitted for stroke treatment is highly skewed. In this particular data set, the vast majority of patients remained in the hospital for only one, two, or three days, but some remained for much longer. The shape of the distribution was highly skewed with a peak at the low end and a long tail extending to much higher values. As a result, the mean, which is highly influenced by outliers, was higher than the typical number of days that patients stayed in the hospital.

Several hospitals had mean lengths of stay that were much greater than most, extending as high as 20 days. What could possibly be going on at these hospitals to cause such extended stays? I immediately suspected the cause: means of small data sets are much more susceptible to outliers than those of large data sets. For example, a tiny hospital that only treats 10 stroke patients in the year will have an excessively high mean length of stay if a single patient had an uncharacteristically long stay. Nine of the patients could have stayed in the hospital from one to three days, but if a single patient remained in the hospital for half a year, the mean length of stay would be in the 20-day range. This same outlier would have much less influence on the mean in a hospital that treated 100 stroke patients during the year, likely resulting in a mean that is less than four. A quick look at the data confirmed that all of the hospitals that had long average lengths of stay were small and therefore treated relatively few stroke patients during the year.

Means are appropriate measures of central tendency only when the distribution is normal. When distributions aren't normal, the median is a better measure of central tendency. Unfortunately, all of the competitors accepted means without question, resulting in imaginative interpretations of patient behavior and hospital errors.

Knowing the proper level and method of aggregation requires training and experience, rooted in statistics.

Expression of the Data

The Question: "Is it appropriate for the quantitative values to be expressed in these particular ways?"

Quantitative values can be expressed in multiple units of measure. Consider the seemingly simple example of sales revenues. We could express revenues in U.S. dollars. If the revenues were generated in the United Kingdom, we could express them as either GBP (i.e., pounds sterling) or convert them to U.S. dollars, which is often done by international companies. We could also express them as percentages of total sales. If a currency conversion is done, we could base the conversion on the conversion rate at the exact time of the sale or perform a less precise conversion, such as one that's based on the conversion rate as of the end of the sales month. We might also choose to express revenues as a rate, such as the rate of increase or decrease compared to the previous period (e.g., this month's revenues compared to last month's). All of these expressions of the measure are potentially legitimate and useful, but not for all purposes. We should take care to always express measures in ways that fit the task at hand.

When we base decisions on understanding that we've woven from data, we cannot afford to leave any of these questions unanswered. In the next chapter, we'll consider how to think critically and scientifically about metrics.

CHAPTER 5 – MEASURE WISELY

Two of the questions that we frequently ask when trying to understand the world are "How many?" and "How much?" We answer these questions by measuring things: either by counting them or by using an instrument (a yardstick, thermometer, Geiger counter, etc.) to compare them to a standard unit of measure (inches, degrees Celsius, rads, etc.). The popular term *metric* is merely a synonym for *measure* although it tends to refer more narrowly to matters of performance, especially those that we consider important (e.g., *key performance metrics*). The term metric sounds cooler and lends an air of gravitas, but metrics are just numbers that we use to quantify counts and amounts, keep track of them, and, ideally, make sense of them. When we count the number of people in a classroom to determine how current attendance compares to past attendance, we're using a metric. When we use a measuring cup to determine the correct amount of sugar for a cake, we're relying on a metric. We've been using metrics since our ancient ancestors began using their fingers to count things. There's nothing magical or mysterious about metrics, but they play an important role in data sensemaking.

Most of what we examine in our efforts to understand what's going on in our organizations are metrics that we deem vital to our strategic objectives. Unfortunately, our focus on metrics often degenerates into a mindless obsession. Metrics are frequently misunderstood, misapplied, and endowed with messianic significance. Most organizations haven't a clue what they should be measuring or how. In concept, metrics are utterly simple, so it's a travesty when they're pursued ineffectively. Jerry Z. Muller has written a wonderful and timely book, *The Tyranny of Metrics*, which puts metrics into perspective.

While we are bound to live in an age of measurement, we live

in an age of mismeasurement, over-measurement, misleading
measurement, and counter-productive measurement.[1]

We can and should learn to think critically and scientifically about
metrics. In the 19th century, the physicist Lord Kelvin declared:

> *When you can measure what you are speaking about, and*
> *express it in numbers, you know something about it; but*
> *when you cannot express it in numbers, your knowledge is of*
> *a meager and unsatisfactory kind; it may be the beginning of*
> *knowledge, but you have scarcely in your thoughts advanced*
> *to the state of science.[2]*

A core assumption that helped to shape the development of science
is that, if you can measure something, you can understand it.
During the last years of the 20th century, expressions such as "what
gets measured gets done" began to show up in popular books and
articles about management. Today, everyone talks about metrics as
vital, but few use them effectively.

   In his clever and practical book *How to Measure Anything*,
Douglas Hubbard convincingly argues that we can measure
anything that we can observe, but that doesn't mean we *should*
measure everything that can be measured. Given the vast field of
possibility, we must learn how to identify the metrics that are most
useful, how to quantify them, and how to use them to promote
desired outcomes.

Select the Right Metrics

In 1963, William Bruce Cameron wrote:

> *Not everything that can be counted counts.*
> *Not everything that counts can be counted.[3]*

Metrics are not a panacea. Hubbard encourages restraint.

> *In business cases, only a few key variables merit deliberate*
> *measurement efforts. The rest of the variables have an*
> *"information value" at or near zero.[4]*

To derive value from metrics, we must first identify which metrics are worthwhile. According to Alan Gregg:

> *Most of the knowledge and much of the genius of the research worker lie behind his selection of what is worth observing. It is a crucial choice, often determining the success or failure of months of work, often differentiating the brilliant discoverer from the...plodder.*[5]

To avoid measuring aimlessly, we must begin by thinking critically about our organization's purpose and objectives. What are we trying to do? Why is it important? Only metrics that help us serve our purpose and achieve our objectives are useful, and only those objectives that produce real benefits are worth pursuing. We shouldn't measure simply because we can. We should measure what matters.

Metrics can be used for various purposes. For example, scientists use them to advance understanding, not necessarily to inform particular decisions and actions. As data sensemakers, however, we focus on metrics that can be leveraged to produce useful outcomes. We want our organizations or the world at large to benefit in some manner. We strive to create desirable outcomes by setting objectives and striving to achieve them. Our metrics should focus on those realms of understanding that most help us achieve our objectives. As our objectives change to address changing circumstances, our metrics should change accordingly.

Stacey Barr is one of the few true experts in the use of performance metrics. In her marvelous book *Prove It!*, she addresses the selection of metrics:

> *Often in measuring a goal we ask a question—"So, how do we measure that?'—too soon. As soon as we answer that question, we're doomed. The measures will be trivial counts, milestones, measures from the past, data we know we already have, the easy stuff to measure, and vague concepts that sound impressive but no-one knows how to quantify. And all these measures will have little to no strength in convincing us whether the goal is truly achieved.*[6]

Before thinking about how we might measure something, we should thoughtfully focus on identifying the metrics that will provide the most useful understanding for achieving our objectives. This begins by identifying and clarifying the objectives that will most effectively set us on the path to fulfilling our mission.

> *Let's say we want to measure innovation. Innovation is a concept, it's not even a goal. A goal for innovation might be "build a climate and culture of innovation." This goal isn't clear and it isn't measurable. What exactly is a climate and culture of innovation? How is a climate different to a culture? What exactly is innovation? Perhaps this goal means that people feel motivated or compelled to generate and test ideas that bring about leaps rather than tweaks in any area of business performance. This is the first step: rewriting the goal to say what we really mean.[7]*

People too often propose metrics that aren't worthwhile. As data sensemakers, we should discourage useless metrics. Here's a question that I routinely ask clients who want to focus on metrics that I suspect are of little or no use: "Can you give me an example of when this metric would lead you to do something in response, and, furthermore, can you describe what that response would be?" If they can't come up with a valid example and explain how they would respond, they might suddenly realize for themselves that the metric isn't worthwhile.

It would be all too easy to simply measure what we're told to measure and leave it at that. It's easy, but it's also wrong. In their book *What the Numbers Say*, Derrick Niederman and David Boyum point out that useful metrics always answer useful questions:

> *A number only gets to be useful when considered as the answer to a question. To be a good consumer of numbers, the reader must constantly ask himself:*
>
> - *To what question is this number (supposed to be) the answer?*
> - *Is it the correct answer to that question?*
> - *Is that the question to which I need an answer?[8]*

Understanding quantitative information always hinges on asking the right questions.

Even when our objectives are clear, we often err by asking questions about the activities that we engage in to achieve our objectives rather than about the objectives themselves—the desired outcomes. According to Barr, "We focus too much on measuring what we do, not the results of what we do."[9] We tend to measure inputs rather than outputs, things that we do, rather than their outcomes, symptoms rather than root causes.

> *We're good at treating symptoms, but symptoms return as soon as we back the treatment off. In business, the treatment is often more of something: more people, more hours, more money, more expectations. This isn't improving performance; it's compensating for lack of performance.*[10]

For instance, a sales team might set a particular number of customer contacts as its goal and then focus on counting the number of times that salespeople interact with their customers. Does a high number of interactions with customers necessarily indicate a good outcome? It doesn't. It's obvious that it doesn't, but it's easy to count customer contacts, so it's a popular metric.

This hints at another common problem: inappropriate *proxies* (a.k.a., surrogates). In the realm of metrics, a proxy is a measure of something other than, but in some way related to, the actual outcome that we're trying to achieve. We hope that by measuring the proxy we'll learn something significant and useful about the actual outcome that we care about, but proxies often fail to enlighten.

It's easy to choose inadequate proxies when we lose sight of the strategic objective that a metric is supposed to address and act as though the proxy is the actual thing of interest. There is a logical fallacy associated with this called *proof surrogate*: a claim that masquerades as proof or evidence when none has been offered. For example, classroom attendance, although important in education, is not an adequate proxy for optimal learning outcomes.

Let's consider a business example. Companies often measure revenues as a proxy for financial success. However, if revenues are increased by increasing expenses to an equal or greater degree, we aren't benefiting financially. We can test the appropriateness of a proxy by asking the question, "Is it possible for this proxy to improve while the thing that we actually care about is not improving?" For example, "Is it possible for revenues to increase while the financial health of the company is remaining the same or declining?" It is indeed possible. Asking a question like this is an example of thinking critically and scientifically with data, attempting to disprove our own hypothesis that increasing revenues indicate financial success.

We tend to prefer measuring what's easy to measure. We crave ease, even when the work is inherently hard, and simplicity, even when faced with complexity. The Deepwater Horizon oil drilling disaster occurred, in part, because British Petroleum (BP) and the company that owned the drilling rig, Transocean, focused on safety metrics that were easy to track, such as holding hand rails and keeping lids on coffee cups. The actual risks that led to the disaster were embedded in the overwhelming complexities of drilling to such great depths, which would have been much more difficult to understand and manage but which posed much greater hazards than slipping or spilling hot coffee. Even after the disaster, Transocean wrote the following bit of self-serving nonsense in a securities filing:

> *Notwithstanding the tragic loss of life in the Gulf of Mexico, we achieved an exemplary statistical safety record as measured by our total recordable incident rate and total potential severity rate...As measured by these standards, we recorded the best year in safety performance in our company's history, which is a reflection on our commitment to achieving an incident-free environment.*[11]

Transocean demonstrated a clear lack of critical thinking, which they later sought to mask. A greater commitment to safety would have led them to measure what mattered, regardless of difficulty. A company that is only willing to track the simple stuff (e.g., keeping lids on coffee cups) should only build and operate simple systems.

When determining the right metrics, we should not assign a disproportionate weight to trivial issues. This tendency reveals biases and logical fallacies that go by names such as the *law of triviality, Parkinson's law,* and *bikeshedding.* These explain why an organization might choose to avoid complexities, such as those involved in designing a nuclear reactor, and instead focus on something easy to grasp or rewarding to the average participant, such as the design of a bike shed on the company's property (thus the name *bikeshedding*).

We often rely on proxies because the data that's needed to directly measure the actual outcome that interests us is not available. The ideal response to this situation is to collect the data that's needed rather than substituting something else for it. If it will take time to put this data collection process in place and accrue enough data to begin the work of sensemaking, it might be appropriate to use a proxy temporarily, as a stopgap measure. Too often, however, proxies that ought to function as stopgaps become permanent, but never adequate, solutions.

We can't always avoid proxies. We often don't have a choice. The outcomes that we care about cannot always be observed directly, no matter how much we try or how creatively we think. For instance, how can we measure employee satisfaction? There's no device that we can attach to an employee's head to measure this. We must rely on proxies, despite the inherent uncertainty that results. For example, we might measure employee turnover as a proxy. Alternatively, we might conduct employee surveys, relying on employees' subjective assessments.

When we must rely on proxies, we should choose them with care and never forget that they are limited stand-ins for the real outcome of interest. Even though proxies are imperfect, they are better than nothing if they significantly reduce our uncertainty. When we use them, we should do so tentatively, periodically circling back to ask whether conditions have changed in a way that would enable us to more directly measure the actual outcome that interests us.

There is an insidious myth that encourages us to choose metrics haphazardly, which has increased in its influence in the last decade;

the myth that, with Big Data, it costs almost nothing to collect and process every bit of data possible. This lie serves the interests of the technology vendors that sell the products and services that are needed to collect, house, and process all of that data. These products and services cost a great deal. Although it's true that the cost of computer hardware, such as storage devices and processors, has decreased over time, what we pay for it hasn't necessarily decreased overall because, as prices come down, we often increase the number of these devices that we buy to such a degree that the costs actually go up. This is especially true when we take into account all of the related costs associated with the purchase, installation, management, and maintenance of these devices and processes. These costs are not trivial.

The ill-begotten mission, *collect everything*, is the sibling of *measure everything.* Jerry Muller asks and then answers an important question about costs:

> *What are the costs of acquiring the metrics? Information is never free, and often it is expensive in ways that rarely occur to those who demand more of it...Every moment you or your colleagues or employees are devoting to the production of metrics is time not devoted to the activities being measured.*[12]

Most of an organization's efforts should be expended on actually doing the work that's directly related to the organization's purpose, which rarely involves information technology (IT). Much of the money that we spend on IT could be better spent to directly support the organization's core objectives. Measuring what doesn't need to be measured results in lost opportunities. Now that's a metric that matters— opportunities lost because of excessive expenditures on IT—but it's seldom measured.

What we measure determines what we do. Measuring things that aren't vital to what we do is a distraction. It's easy to lose sight of our goals as we focus on useless metrics. What's not measured is soon ignored. Finding the right metrics is vital.

Think Quantitatively

Good metrics are the products of good quantitative thinking. Notice that I didn't say that they're the products of advanced mathematics. Only basic mathematics are required for most data sensemaking. According to Niederman and Boyum, "Being a good quantitative thinker requires little math beyond six grade levels."[13] Their assessment matches my own experience. I only studied introductory geometry and introductory algebra in middle school and, because my algebra teacher was awful, I never developed an interest in mathematics. Later, as college student, I only took a single introductory course in statistics but eventually went on to read several introductory to intermediate-level books about statistics on my own. Although I might have been enriched in many ways by further studies in mathematics and statistics, I've rarely needed more than the basics in my work as a data sensemaker. I know the limits of my statistical knowledge and gladly turn to others for help when I need it. I'm not saying that more advanced mathematics isn't needed for some data-sensemaking tasks—it certainly is, especially when supporting science and engineering activities—but the data sensemaking that's needed to support most organizations most of the time requires only basic math.

The math that's required primarily involves addition, subtraction, multiplication, and division, which is why Niederman and Boyum specified a sixth-grade level of education. The statistics that are required consist mostly of understanding measures of central tendency and variation (e.g., means, medians, minimums, maximums, and percentiles). Also fundamental to data sensemaking is knowing how to represent quantitative information graphically to find and examine meaningful patterns and relationships in the data (e.g., the shape of variation through time, the shape of a variable's distribution from its lowest the highest values, or the shape of the relationship between two quantitative variables). These basics are relatively easy to learn, but they are not intuitive. They require study and practice.

It's worthwhile to note that statistics can be broken down into two fundamental types: *descriptive* and *predictive* (a.k.a., inferential). The purpose of descriptive statistics is to understand quantitative behavior—what has happened. The purpose of predictive statistics is to anticipate quantitative behavior in the future given specific conditions—what will likely happen. Most of the data sensemaking that we typically engage in is descriptive in nature and does not require an advanced understanding of statistics. However, it's important to realize that we cannot venture far into the realm of predictive statistics without advanced training. To predict the probability of particular outcomes, we must build statistical models, and that requires more than the basics. We must know our limits and rely on others with more advanced statistical training when we need to understand the probabilities of what might happen rather than just the actualities of what has happened.

The best introduction to basic quantitative thinking that I've encountered is the book *What the Numbers Say* by Derrick Niederman and David Boyum, which I've mentioned already. The best general introduction to statistical thinking that I've read is the book *Naked Statistics* by Charles Wheelan. It's wonderfully accessible and practical. I wish these books had been available in the early days of my work as a data sensemaker. They would have saved me a lot of time and prevented me from making numerous errors. For an introduction to the basic principles and practices of data visualization, I recommend my own books *Show Me the Numbers* and *Now You See It*.

In addition to basic quantitative thinking skills, some additional skills specific to effective measurement are useful as well. I recommend two books in particular that introduce these skills: *How to Measure Anything*, by Douglas Hubbard, and *Prove It!*, by Stacey Barr.

Measure at the Right Level

Metrics are only useful when they're associated with the right categories and expressed at the right level. It might be interesting and somewhat informative to track a company's profit margin overall, but if profits are down, we won't know what to do about them unless we know which specific products or regions contribute to low profit margins. Our profit margin might look great overall, but it could be extremely low for particular products or in particular regions without our knowledge if we aggregated revenues solely at the company level. Aggregating at too general a level is a common mistake.

Metrics are only useful if they measure what's going on within homogeneous groups. Items that we examine as a group should be alike. Their characteristics, at least those that potentially have an influence on the metric that we're examining, should be shared. If the items that we've grouped together exhibit significant diversity—heterogeneity—we can't use metrics meaningfully to describe their behavior. Diverse behaviors, when aggregated, can cancel one another out, resulting in a description that describes nothing meaningfully. Consider a simple example. Let's say we want to examine the metric of people's heights, such as the heights of people in a particular profession in which height matters, like the sport of basketball. If we group men and women together, an aggregate of their heights, such as the median, would not at all describe the group as a whole. It would fall somewhere in between the median heights of men and women. It would make more sense to examine men and women separately, which would allow us to determine the typical heights in a manner that would indeed characterize those specific groups.

Imagine that we work for a hospital and want to measure patient outcomes to determine whether we're treating our patients effectively. To understand this, should we group all patients together, regardless of their sex or age, and regardless of their illnesses or the specific treatments that they received? We should not. Let's just focus on one aspect of this for the moment: the nature of the medical treatment. When considering patient outcomes, can we group treatments that involve surgeries in with those that only involve medicines? It wouldn't make sense to do this because the potential risks and outcomes of these treatments are quite different. This measurement problem is even more complicated than the example has so far revealed. For example, even if we focus solely on surgical outcomes, can we treat all surgeries the same? Doing so would not likely produce a useful result because surgeries are done for different reasons and have widely varying risks and potential benefits. We might want to improve patient outcomes overall, but our efforts to do this will need to focus on specific, homogeneous groups. Metrics associated with heterogeneous groups are of little value.

When considering the right level of aggregation, perhaps no category concerns us more than time. At what interval of time should we examine the metric: annually, quarterly, monthly, weekly, daily, hourly? If the level of aggregation is too general, important signals in the behavior of that metric as it changes through time will escape our notice. On the other hand, aggregating the metric at too fine a level will create a problem if behavior at that level is erratic. For example, monitoring sales revenues at a daily level usually wouldn't make sense because sales jump around too much from day to day. Those daily changes are rarely meaningful. For this reason, we typically monitor sales at a weekly or monthly level, which will more likely reveal significant changes in behavior when they occur. When determining the right level of aggregation, we're looking for the sweet spot, the Goldilocks zone: not too big, not too small, but just right.

Avoid Common Measurement Errors

People make a number of common statistical mistakes when constructing metrics. Let's consider a few of these errors.

Inappropriate Use of the Mean

Perhaps foremost among the measurement problems that I've encountered is misuse of the *mean* as a measure of central tendency (i.e., what's typical). As I've already mentioned, the mean was specifically and solely designed as a measure of central tendency for *normal distributions*—those that are bell-shaped with a peak in the middle. A histogram of a normal distribution looks something like this:

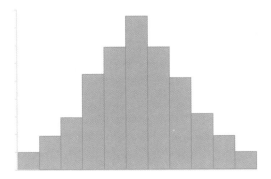

The mean does not represent the value that's typical for distributions that are shaped differently. The distribution of annual household income in America illustrates this. It's skewed with a long tail that extends far out to the right toward greater wealth. For example, the 2013 mean annual household income of $72,641 did not accurately represent what was typical. Using the mean as the metric for tracking income in America isn't appropriate. The mean household income can actually increase while most American household incomes remain the same or even decline.

What's typical is better represented by a different measure of central tendency: the *median*. As a general rule of thumb for most data-sensemaking purposes, we should use the median as the measure of central tendency.

Sole Reliance on Measures of Central Tendency

Measures of central tendency don't tell the full story of a variable's distribution. In addition to a measure of central tendency, two other characteristics are needed, at a minimum, to understand the nature of a distribution: the *spread* (i.e., the lowest and highest values, as well as the distance between them) and the *shape*. The median could remain the same while the spread or the shape of the distribution changed significantly. Going back to the example of household income, the median could remain constant while many people become poorer. We would never know this if we relied solely on the median household income. To keep these other aspects of income in mind, we might need a combination of metrics, such as the median, minimum, maximum, 25th percentile, and 75th percentile. A change in any one of these metrics could reveal something significant.

Conflating Rankings with Measures of Worth

Even though rankings are based on quantitative measures, they are not quantitative themselves. Rather, they are ordinal. They merely arrange a set of categorical items in order based on some quantitative measure that's associated with those items. For example, we might order a list of students, from high to low, based on their test scores. Rankings reveal relative performance solely in an ordinal manner, not quantitatively. Just because Suzie is ranked number one on an exam does not necessarily mean that she did well on it (for example, if all the students including Suzie got less than 50% of the answers correct), just as James' last-place ranking does not necessarily mean he did poorly (for example, if all the students scored 90% or better).

Rankings also mislead us if we assume that the distances in relative performance between consecutive items are equal to one another. This isn't the case. The top performer could be considerably better than the second-place performer, who could be only slightly better than the third-place performer. Even when we recognize this limitation intellectually, it's still easy to misread rankings in this way.

Similarly, we err when we assume that focusing on the top or bottom few items in a ranked list (e.g., the top or bottom 10) necessarily makes sense. Imagine a ranked list of items in which the top eight items exhibit nearly equal performance, but then the ninth performs significantly worse. If we want to focus on the top performers in this case, it would make more sense to consider the top eight items, not the top ten.

Rankings can certainly be informative at times but are rarely the basis for a useful metric. It usually works best to consider rankings in association with the quantitative values on which they are based rather than on their own.

Monitor Effectively

Once we've identified a metric and figured out how to quantify it properly, we can monitor it to observe how it changes. Typically, we want a metric to either remain within a desired range or to move in a particular direction and perhaps to a particular degree. A metric's value will almost always vary to some degree over time, but not all variation is significant. Variation within the range that's routine indicates business as usual. By contrast, we see a potential signal that something in the underlying process has perhaps changed when variation 1) exceeds the threshold of routine behavior, either above or below; 2) moves consistently in one direction over several intervals of time; or 3) remains either above or below average for several intervals of time in a row. If it changes in the wrong direction, we want to identify the cause and do what we can to fix it. If it changes in the right direction, we want to identify the cause and do what we can to encourage it.

We determine the range of routine variation using statistical methods. By observing how values have changed over an extended period of time, we can determine the range within which values usually fall. For instance, we can determine the range within which 95% of the values fall, with specific lower and upper boundaries. A value is either exceptionally low or exceptionally high when it falls outside of those boundaries. As an example, we might determine that the number of daily defects in a particular manufacturing process dips below three or exceeds nine only 5% of the time. While it is certainly possible that values in these extreme ranges occur by chance, an extreme value deserves to be investigated as a possible signal that something unusual is occurring due to an identifiable cause.

What I'm describing here in general is a method called *Statistical Process Control (SPC)*, which originally grew out of the work of Walter Shewhart. He made an important distinction between two types of variation: 1) routine variation—what's expected unless something has changed, and 2) exceptional variation—what's outside the bounds of routine and is therefore a potential signal. Shewhart created the *control chart* (a.k.a., *process control chart*) to graphically distinguish these two types of variation.

I mentioned earlier that we often want a metric's value to move in a particular direction over time, and perhaps to a particular degree. I was alluding to targets—specific thresholds that we hope to achieve. Targets can serve as useful goals, but not if they are arbitrarily determined. Unfortunately, many of the targets that organizations establish are mere wishes, not realistic assessments of what's achievable. An annual goal of increasing revenues by 20% is a fantasy and a millstone around our necks if we don't know how to achieve it. As data sensemakers, we can help our organizations set achievable goals by using methods such as SPC to determine realistic expectations and then identify specific steps to produce desired changes. We can encourage people to keep their hopes tied to reality and to focus their efforts on actions that are aligned with known causes of the outcomes that they desire. In other words, we can help people think critically and scientifically about targets.

Respond Effectively

Once a metric has been identified, the method of quantifying it has been devised, and the process of monitoring it has been established, we should use the metric with care. Metrics can be and often are used unwisely, and in harmful ways. When properly used, metrics provide the understanding that we need to do something better. That understanding should be used to enable those who are in a position to respond; rarely to reward or punish. Metrics don't usually produce desired outcomes when they're used to motivate people using carrots or sticks.

Jerry Muller describes the risk of using metrics as rewards:

> *Many of the problems of pay-for-performance schemes can be traced to an overly simple, indeed deeply distortive, conception of human motivation, one that assumes that people are motivated to work only by material rewards…In general, extrinsic rewards—pay-for-performance, incentives pay, bonuses—are most effective in commercial organizations, where the primary goal is to make money. They also work well when the task to be completed is discrete, easily measured, and not of much intrinsic interest, such as the*

*production of some standardized good on an assembly line…
But when mission-oriented organizations try to use extrinsic
rewards,…the result may actually be counterproductive. The
use of extrinsic rewards for activities of high intrinsic interest
leads people to focus on the rewards and not on the intrinsic
interest of the task, or on the larger mission of which it is a
part. The result is a "crowding out" of intrinsic motivation:
having been taught to think of their work tasks primarily as
a means toward monetary goals, they lose interest in doing
the work for the sake of a larger mission of the institution.
Alternatively, they may perceive the offer of payment for
performance as an insult to their professional ethics, and
indeed to their self-esteem, implying that they are in it for the
money.[14]*

Research has shown that using metrics to reward or punish
rarely has a significant effect on the outcomes. Furthermore, using
metrics in this manner can lead to misinformation as people learn
to game the system. What happens when you punish doctors who
treat the most complicated cases for failing to produce outcomes
that are only possible for less complicated cases? Doctors sometimes
respond by refusing to treat the complicated cases. Ben Orlin
illustrated the problem in his entertaining and enlightening book
Math with Bad Drawings.

(Image courtesy of Ben Orlin. 2018. *Math with Bad Drawings,* New York, NY: Black
Dog & Leventhal Publishers, p. 259.)

What happens when hospitals are compared to one another by ranking them based on reported metrics, resulting in the shaming of hospitals that are ranked poorly? Many figure out how to fudge the data, resulting in misinformation, which renders the metric useless. Sometimes the hospitals that are doing the best work are ranked among the poorest simply because they're the only ones that are reporting the data honestly. When hospital readmission rates became a popular metric that was used to shame hospitals with high rates, regardless of the reason, many hospitals came up with ways to cheat. According to Muller, "Instead of formally admitting returning patients, hospitals place them on 'observation status,' under which the patient stays in the hospital for a period of time (up to several days), and is billed for outpatient services rather than a readmission."[15]

Carrots and sticks can also discourage creativity.

> *Trying to force people to conform their work to preestablished numerical goals tends to stifle innovation and creativity—valuable qualities in most settings. And it almost inevitably leads to a valuation of short-term goals over long-term purposes.*[16]

When a metric is used as a bludgeon, people do what they can to avoid or undermine it. Who could blame them?

Metrics are usually embraced when people find them genuinely useful. This occurs more often when the people who are made responsible for metrics are involved in selecting and constructing those metrics and know how to respond to them productively. We should do everything in our power to make sure that these conditions exist.

Metrics are often used to enforce accountability, but accountability is only appropriate when people can actually achieve that for which they're held accountable. According to the management theorist W. Edwards Deming:

> *How could there be life without aims and hopes? Everyone has aims, hopes, plans. But a goal that lies beyond the means of accomplishment will lead to discouragement,*

frustration, demoralization. In other words, there must be a method to achieve an aim.[17]

When the methods that are needed to achieve our objectives aren't clear, we can collaborate with the folks who work in the trenches to search for solutions. We can look for potential causes, form hypotheses, and devise simple experiments to test those hypotheses, all the while tracking the data to determine whether our efforts succeed and then adjusting the metrics as needed. When we combine our strengths in data sensemaking with the complementary strengths of more experienced domain experts, we become enablers and will be embraced more readily as trusted partners. When metrics are used in this manner, they enlighten and empower.

CHAPTER 6 – DEVELOP GOOD
THINKING HABITS

To be successful weavers of understanding from data, we need to not only develop the *thinking skills* outlined in this book but also develop good *thinking habits*. It's easy for our minds to become cluttered and hobbled in ways that interfere with sound thinking. Fortunately, we can cultivate three habits to keep our minds clear and fully engaged in the task at hand: prevent distraction, take notes, and sleep on it.

Prevent Distraction

We live in a world of increasing distractions. Our thoughts are constantly being pulled here and there, often in ways that divert concentration from the task at hand. Our ability to narrowly focus attention on a single task contributed to our evolutionary advantage, but it remains subject to interruption by perceived threats or opportunities. During a hunt on the African savannah in the early days of our species, relatively little existed in our environment to distract us from focusing on our prey. Having our attention grabbed by the occasional appearance of a predator or a better food source served a worthwhile purpose: survival. Now, in the modern world, perceived threats and opportunities abound, but few have any real bearing our survival. Every ping of our smartphones suggests an opportunity that we are powerless to resist. Attentional switching from one point of focus to another, such as from data sensemaking to an incoming text message, comes with a significant cost. Once our attention shifts, it takes a great deal of time to get it back on track. According to Gloria Mark of the University of California, Irvine, it takes about 25 minutes, on average, to get fully back on task after an interruption. Our brains work best when we can keep them focused on the task at hand unless another task arises that is genuinely more important.

We can combat distractions, in part, by creating an environment that is designed to resist them. When we want to think deeply, it helps to have a quiet place with little in our perceptual field other than the data and the tools that we're using to make sense of it. This means that we must turn off the auditory and visual alerts that are emitted by our electronic devices. We should shut down all windows on our screens other than those that support the task at hand. We might also need to close the office door, if we're lucky enough to have one, with a sign clearly posted to discourage interruptions.

The need for managing the many distractions that have proliferated since the advent of electronic communications, entertainment, and social media is getting increasing attention these days. Many books and articles have now been written on the topic, not by technophobes but by technologists who intimately understand the risks. One of the best books that I've read on the topic is *Deep Work: Rules for Focused Success in a Distracted World* by Cal Newport.

Newport focuses on the needs of knowledge workers and advocates *deep work*, which he defines in the following way:

> *Deep Work: Professional activities performed in a state of distraction-free concentration that push your cognitive capabilities to their limit. These efforts create new value, improve your skill, and are hard to replicate.[1]*

Newport proposes the following formula: high-quality work produced = time spent x intensity of focus. I agree. He makes a convincing case.

> *The ubiquity of deep work among influential individuals is important to emphasize because it stands in sharp contrast to the behavior of most modern knowledge workers—a group that's rapidly forgetting the value of going deep.*

> *The reason knowledge workers are losing familiarity with deep work is well established: network tools. This is a broad*

*category that captures communication services like e-mail
and SMS, social media networks like Twitter and Facebook,
and the shiny tangle of infotainment sites like BuzzFeed and
Reddit. In aggregate, the rise of these tools, combined with
ubiquitous access to them through smartphones and
networked office computers, has fragmented most knowledge
workers' attention into slivers. A 2012 McKinsey study found
that the average knowledge worker now spends more than 60
percent of the workweek engaged in electronic communication
and Internet searching, with close to 30 percent of a worker's
time dedicated to reading and answering e-mail alone.[2]*

Newport also recognizes how difficult it can be to combat the forces
that make deep work rare and its importance unrecognized.

*Deep work is at a severe disadvantage in a technopoly
because it builds on values like quality, craftsmanship, and
mastery that are decidedly old-fashioned and nontechno-
logical. Even worse, to support deep work often requires the
rejection of much of what is new and high-tech. Deep work is
exiled in favor of more distracting high-tech behaviors, like
the professional use of social media, not because the former is
empirically inferior to the latter. Indeed, if we had hard
metrics relating the impact of these behaviors on the bottom
line, our current technopoly would likely crumble.[3]*

Those of us who work as data sensemakers need to engage in deep
work routinely, not in rare spurts. Rather than scheduling special
times for deep work, we should instead pursue it routinely and
schedule occasional breaks.

It makes sense, ordinarily, to set aside entire days for deep work,
with only brief periods at the beginning and end of the work day
for administrative activities (e.g., handling emails), and to take
occasional breaks during the day to relax and daydream. I take
walks—at least two each day without fail—to stretch my legs and
allow my mind to wander. Deep work requires extended periods of
consistent effort, uninterrupted by meaningless activities that pull

the mind from concentration, but it can't be sustained without occasional breaks.

Neuroscientists refer to the daydreaming state as the *default mode*. This is because daydreaming is the most natural state of the brain. In any moment, our brains are either in the resting state of daydreaming or attentively engaged in a task, never both at the same time. Even without a specific distraction that hijacks our attention from the task at hand, our brains can easily shift into default mode without notice. Our minds are prone to wander because it's less cognitively taxing. Entire disciplines such as *mindfulness meditation* have been developed to manage this tendency. Developing the ability to maintain attention is quite useful for our lives in general, not solely for our professional lives.

Daydreaming isn't necessarily bad—it actually serves a number of useful purposes—it just isn't what's usually needed when we're trying to make sense of data. Without discipline, most of us shift into the default mode seamlessly and often, without intention or control. When this happens, we should simply shift our attention back to the task at hand. Eliminating distractions in our environment helps us do this. Scheduling periodic daydreaming breaks during the day to relax and refresh our minds also helps because concentration takes energy, which is not boundless.

In addition to refreshing our minds, daydreaming breaks can also contribute more directly to data sensemaking by enabling a creative mode that can't be achieved through focused, deliberate, logical, linear, and methodical thinking. Working diligently with data to make sense of it isn't always productive. This narrow focus can work against us at times, making it hard to see the forest for the trees. On these occasions, a little distance can be useful. Allowing our minds to wander can open our awareness to connections in the data that would be difficult to find through focused attention. This works especially well when our minds have already been primed with a number of facts and questions that we've accumulated through hours or even days of attentive data sensemaking. The facts are there, but meaningful connections among them will sometimes only surface while daydreaming. Some of my greatest insights have emerged when, after struggling to make sense of something for a while without success, I take a walk or soak in the tub and allow my mind to wander. Suddenly, the pieces fall into place. Not always, but often. This can only happen during daydreaming if the hard work of focused attention precedes it. For this reason, it makes sense to engage in deep work as the norm and daydreaming as an occasional exception.

Unless we've developed a great deal of mental discipline through practices such as mindfulness meditation—something I've yet to accomplish— our minds will still wander from our work from time to time even after we've eliminated most distractions. Other parts of our lives creep into our awareness. These are often little concerns, such as a leaky faucet or some upsetting event in the news, and they're difficult to shake. Sometimes these moments of distraction produce ideas that are useful but unrelated to our work (e.g., "I should replace the batteries in the smoke alarms."), so we don't want to lose them, but we also don't want to continue ruminating on them while trying to work. What can we do? The best response is to write those ideas down for later reference. David Allen, the author of *Getting Things Done*, calls this kind of note-taking *clearing the mind*. Doing this frees us to shift back into focusing on the task at hand without worrying that something important will be forgotten. If we try to hold these thoughts in memory rather than writing them down, our minds will come back to them again and again, periodically rehearsing them in an effort to remember. Taking notes can support our data-sensemaking efforts in other ways as well, which is our next topic.

Take Notes

The usefulness of note-taking extends beyond extraneous thoughts that distract us while we're trying to focus. It's also useful for recording relevant insights that we develop during the data-sensemaking process. Writing things down serves as an external form of memory that remains one of the most powerful technologies of human history. The combination of pen or pencil and paper is one of the most useful technologies ever developed for thinking critically and scientifically with data. In fact, one of the best methods involves slips of paper, such as 3x5 inch index cards, that are always on hand for jotting down ideas for later reference. These cards can be arranged and grouped in various ways to support thinking. Alternatives, such as digital applications for recording and organizing notes can also be useful, but only if they're simple to use.

When we work in collaboration with other data sensemakers, our notes can be shared with the entire team. If we work together in the same physical space, recording thoughts on a whiteboard or on large pieces of paper posted on the wall can be effective. When we don't share the same physical space, a shared repository of electronic notes usually works best. When our data-sensemaking tool provides a convenient means of recording notes in the tool itself, in the form of annotations to the data, this provides a useful way to keep our thoughts tightly coupled to the data that gave rise to them.

For more on the usefulness of note taking and a host of other tips for organizing thoughts, I recommend the book *The Organized Mind*, by Daniel J. Levitin.

Sleep on It

You might think it odd that I'm including a section on the importance of sleep in a book about data sensemaking, but I can assure you, and hope to convince you, that it's perfectly reasonable. Our biological well-being depends primarily on air, water, and food, but also sleep. Every species that has ever been studied sleeps although the degree and composition of sleep varies from creature to creature. Sleep has played an important role in supporting human advancement to the top of the evolutionary heap. Without adequate sleep, our bodies degrade, and our minds falter.

Unfortunately, according to sleep scientists, most of us don't get enough sleep. Matthew Walker, professor of neuroscience and director of the University of California, Berkeley's Sleep and Neuroimaging Lab, warns:

Humans are not sleeping the way nature intended. The number of sleep bouts, the duration of sleep, and when sleep occurs have all been comprehensively distorted by modernity.[4]

A hundred years ago, less than 2 percent of the population in the United States slept six hours or less a night. Now, almost 30 percent of Americans do.[5]

Although rare individuals can function fine on as little as six hours of sleep, most of us need about eight hours of sleep each night. Less-than-adequate sleep is associated with a long list of physical, cognitive, and emotional problems. It might surprise you to learn that, according to Walker, more traffic accidents are caused by sleepiness than by drug and alcohol consumption combined.

Insufficient sleep correlates strongly with a loss in concentration. Given our interest in data sensemaking, we'll focus on two cognitive benefits of sleep in particular: 1) increased memory and learning, and 2) increased problem-solving ability.

Within the brain, sleep enriches a diversity of functions, including our ability to learn, memorize, and make logical decisions and choices. Benevolently servicing our psychological health, sleep recalibrates our emotional brain circuits, allowing us to navigate next-day social and psychological challenges with cool-headed composure. We are even beginning to understand the most impervious and controversial of all conscious experiences: the dream. Dreaming provides a unique suite of benefits to all species fortunate enough to experience it, humans included. Among these gifts are a consoling neurological bath that mollifies painful memories and a virtual reality space in which the brain melds past and present knowledge, inspiring creativity.[6]

Our sleep is divided into several distinct stages, but we'll keep things simple and speak only of the two most fundamental categories: *NREM* (non-rapid eye movement) and *REM* (rapid eye movement) sleep. These two parts of sleep are characterized by different brain activities and serve different functions. Specific to cognition, Walker provides the following overview:

> *When it comes to information processing, think of the wake state principally as reception (experiencing and constantly learning the world around you), NREM sleep as reflection (storing and strengthening those raw ingredients of new facts and skills), and REM sleep as integration (interconnecting these raw ingredients with each other, with all past experiences, and, in so doing, building an ever more accurate model of how the world works, including innovative insights and problem-solving abilities).[7]*

During NREM sleep, the experiences that we had during the day while awake, including attempts to memorize and learn things, are filtered, based on their usefulness, and moved into long-term storage. During REM sleep, these new memories are linked with existing memories, sometimes in rich, abstract, and novel ways.

Earlier, I mentioned the value of daydreaming as a useful way to shift perspective, which can often lead to insights. The dreaming that occurs during REM sleep, in contrast, shifts our perspective much more radically, which can be especially useful when we're faced with novel or complex challenges. Dreaming during REM sleep involves many parts of our brains, but not the part where logical thinking occurs. It's the illogical, hallucinatory nature of our dreams that often allows creative connections to be made that would be difficult to discover while awake. Sleeping on it (or more specifically, dreaming on it) can complement logical thinking in useful ways. Research has shown that we can often struggle during the day in our attempts to solve complex problems with deliberate, logical thinking, but then, after a night of dream-infused sleep, we suddenly recognize solutions.

To make sense of data productively, we must get enough sleep. There's a great deal in modern society that makes sufficient sleep difficult to attain, but there are steps that we can take to restore our natural sleeping habits. I won't cover them here, but I encourage you to develop a richer understanding of sleep, including its importance and maintenance, by reading Matthew Walker's wonderful book *Why We Sleep*.

CHAPTER 7 – DEVELOP A DATA-SENSEMAKING CULTURE

To say that we can improve decision making in our organizations by learning to think critically and scientifically with data is an understatement. The benefits would be staggering. So far, however, most organizations have derived relatively little understanding, and therefore relatively little value, from data. More than intelligence or tools, we need skills. In particular, we need to recognize the value of critical thinking and scientific thinking and commit to their use.

Only when our organizations embrace critical and scientific thinking can data sensemaking approach its potential. Those in power in our organizations must make a commitment to this. I'm not saying that the initial impetus for change must come from the top, but until the folks at the top get on board, there is little hope for success. Most of us who work as data sensemakers don't reside near the top of the power hierarchy, but we can certainly make our case to those who do. We can do this in part by demonstrating the greater insights that only critical and scientific thinking can muster. Until these skills are integrated into the culture, our efforts will remain hobbled.

An organization that doesn't value critical and scientific thinking in general won't value these skills when working with data. These aren't specialty skills; they're fundamental. Daniel Kahneman pointed out in his book *Thinking, Fast and Slow* that all organizations, no matter the enterprise, function primarily as *decision factories*. Whether they sell widgets, provide medical care, run the government, promote justice, or anything else, more than any other activity, they make decisions. With this in mind, every organization should prioritize the development of decision-making skills, and nothing enables effective decision making more than critical and scientific thinking.

Teach Others

As data sensemakers, we must serve, in part, as teachers. Decision makers who rely on our findings cannot function effectively as passive recipients of information; they must be able to think critically and scientifically about those findings themselves. To help them with this, we can do each of the following:

- Focus on substance over style.
- Provide context.
- Emphasize particular data with care.
- Express uncertainty.
- Preserve complexity.
- Teach the basics of statistical thinking.
- Encourage questions.
- Identify errors.

Focus on Substance Over Style

A harmful tendency has developed among many information professionals to dress up the data: to emphasize style over substance, narrative over truth, and novelty over effectiveness. As a result, decision makers sometimes expect to be superficially entertained by data rather than thoughtfully engaged with the unvarnished truth. Many of the ways in which data is often packaged distract from and complicate its meaning, resulting in superficial understanding at best. We should show people that data is too important to trivialize by turning it into a video game, that being dazzled by silly effects (e.g., bright, spinning donut charts) is childish, not professional. The recent emphasis on *data storytelling* has too often reduced data presentation to a set of cheap tricks. Learning from data is serious business. Presenting data in ways that are visually or narratively engaging is fine as long as they don't compromise clarity and truth. We achieve clarity and communicate truth by focusing primarily on substance, not on style.

Unfortunately, to re-establish an air of seriousness, we must confront the trivializing expectations that have taken hold over the past few years. We must show people through examples that, when data is presented in perceptually and cognitively effective ways, they can learn a great deal more. We must remind them that the objective is understanding, not entertainment. To understand data, their brains must engage in thinking, not in admiring fancy visuals.

Provide Context

Data cannot be understood apart from its context. Just as we must examine data in context to make sense of it, we must present it to others in context as well, so they may do the same. Pre-digested and overly summarized data, robbed of its contextual nutrients, is as unhealthy for decision support as overly processed foods are for our bodies. We cannot support decision making by serving a diet consisting almost entirely of nutrient-poor white bread. If we do, our organizations will become feeble.

Emphasize Particular Data with Care

When we present data to others, it makes sense to highlight what's most important. Doing so helps them attend to signals rather than noise. However, to do this properly, we must not exclude other necessary contextual data. We can highlight what's most important without omitting essential supporting data.

Express Uncertainty

Whenever we deal with data, we deal with some level of statistical uncertainty. The conclusions that we draw from data are always probable to some degree, never certain. We must help people understand the ways in which and degree to which our findings are uncertain. We do this, in part, by identifying and explaining the causes of uncertainty, such as incomplete or dirty data. If we know that 5% of the data that ought to exist is missing and that 15% of the remaining data is unreliable because of data entry errors, we should provide this information. We can do this in some cases by expressing measures of uncertainty, such as error margins, directly.

By maintaining a constant awareness of the tentativeness of our conclusions, as is done in science, we remain much more open to the possibility of error. Just as this is healthy for science, it's healthy for all forms of data sensemaking.

Preserve Complexity

In our efforts to express data as simply and clearly as possible, we must never over-simplify. As Einstein said, "Everything should be made as simple as possible, but not simpler." When data contains essential complexities, to omit them is to misinform. "But," you might object, "people won't understand those complexities, so I dare not present them." If people lack the expertise that is needed to understand the complexities that must be understood to do their work, the solution is not to remove the complexities but to instead help people develop the expertise that's required. Organizations that rely on dumbed-down information are dumb organizations. Instead of removing complexities, we should work hard to explain them in ways that people can understand. This can take a great deal of time, effort, and imagination. However, there is no doubt that it's worth it.

Explain the Basics of Statistical Thinking

Most decision makers don't need to be statisticians. However, if they rely on quantitative information to do their jobs, they must be able to think statistically in a few basic ways. The basics that are required are much the same as those that we considered in previous chapters, such as recognizing the effects of randomness and knowing not to rely on measures of central tendency alone to understand the nature of variation.

We can introduce these basics to decision makers in the context of the information that we present to them. If we provide a report that describes the nature of a variable's variation, we can include a complete description of that variation and explain why we've done so rather than reducing that variation to a single summary measure, such as a mean or median. Teaching these principles in the context of the information that we present will make them immediately relevant and perhaps even potentially interesting.

Encourage Questions

People learn when they become engaged with information. They become engaged by asking questions about it, such as:

- What's going on here?
- Why is this happening?
- Why did you present this to me in this way?
- Why didn't you include this other data?

We want decision makers to think with data in the same way that we do when we strive to make sense of it. Some people are naturally inclined to ask questions because they're curious and want to understand. These folks are great clients. When people don't exhibit curiosity, we should encourage them to do so. We can encourage them to ask us questions by asking them questions. Each of the following questions would be worthwhile:

- "Why do you think this is happening?"
- "Is any data missing that would be helpful, and, if so, why?"
- "Can you think of any other way this information could be presented that would help you understand it better?"
- "Do you see anything in this report that might lead you to take action?"

We can also encourage people's curiosity by exhibiting our own. We should never, ever discourage questions. We should never give the impression that we find people's questions annoying and certainly never suggest that we think their questions are dumb. Our clients are in some respects our students. We want them to understand the information that we present as well as we do. Teachers whose students become their peers or eventually even surpass them should be proud.

Identify Errors

No, customers are not always right. Even when they do their jobs extremely well, their grasp of data sensemaking is often incomplete and prone to error. We do harm if we allow their errors to go unnoticed and uncorrected. Good teachers don't fail to provide feedback when their students make errors. To learn, we all need feedback. The sooner errors are corrected, the better. We can't force people to embrace our feedback, but we can do our best to encourage them to do so by providing feedback in understandable, useful, and respectful ways. Those who most resist correction are often those who need it most.

Encourage Constructive Critique

The point above about identifying errors underscores the importance of critique. Just as our clients benefit from having errors in their thinking pointed out, organizations as a whole benefit from a culture that embraces critique. Unfortunately, it's the rare organization that does this beyond lip service. I've found that, even in academia, which should be a citadel of critique, it is in fact often discouraged. This is a shame, for only when people are encouraged to critique the work of others can we benefit from one another's perspectives and expertise.

Critique, properly done, is an act of respect. It shows that we value the work of others. Everyone's work can benefit from critique. People who truly care about their work don't build walls to prevent critique.

We can establish mechanisms to encourage critiques and make them convenient. One of the best ways to encourage others to value critiques of their work is by inviting them to critique our own. To do so is a simple and healthy admission that we aren't perfect, we don't know everything, and we need one another. When people critique our work, we should thank them, but this doesn't mean that we should uncritically embrace what they say. Our goal is to create a culture that embraces critical and scientific thinking. This involves peer review, discussion, and even debate. As long as we are focused on learning and doing our best, not on boosting our egos or belittling the work of others, the debate will remain constructive.

In addition to critiques from our peers, it's also important to have our work reviewed by people who work in different parts of the organization or serve in different roles—outsiders—whose training and domain experience differ significantly from ours. Their contrasting perspectives sometimes allow them to spot problems or uncover insights that escape our notice. When we get too close to something—too deeply entrenched—we can become myopic, subject to groupthink or a fixed mindset. Even though much that outsiders offer might be of little value, often because they lack expertise in our particular domain, real revelations are possible. All domains benefit from the fresh perspectives of outsiders; we sometimes have more to learn from outsiders than from our peers, but many insulate themselves from these perspectives.

Not only is it useful to get feedback from outsiders within the organization, it's also useful to invite fresh sets of eyes from outside our organizations. This can be achieved through the use of consultants, but also less formally by attending events, such as courses or conferences, where we can interact with data sensemakers from other organizations or even from different industries. One of the great benefits that my students have gained from attending my public workshops is the opportunity for interaction with others who do similar work in quite different settings. Watching the eyes of my students light up with fresh insights gained from informal conversations during lunch or after class has always brought me joy.

Create a Risk-Free Zone for Admitting Mistakes

Organizations that encourage critique also encourage people to admit mistakes. These two activities go hand in hand. When errors remain hidden, they can fester and grow, act as blind spots in our understanding, or even worse, breed outright misunderstanding.

We all make mistakes. When we think critically and scientifically, we sometimes tackle complexities and venture into unknown territories that make errors likely. Smart people and organizations learn from their mistakes. People who admit their mistakes should be rewarded, not punished. Granted, someone who continues to make the same mistake over and over shouldn't be praised, but mistakes that lead to learning and better performance should be rewarded.

We love to share our success stories, but some of the most beneficial stories that we can share are of our mistakes. Organizations that think critically and scientifically understand and promote this.

Secure Enough Time and Space

Thinking critically and scientifically takes time. Snap judgments and gut feelings work in some situations but rarely in data sensemaking. Sensemaking requires reflection, and reflection takes time. It has been said that "Genius is nothing but a general aptitude for patience." In a time when speed is revered, our need to take things slowly is rarely appreciated. This needs to change. When our organizations give us time enough to think, it isn't wasted. Demands for instant answers should be recognized as foolish.

One of the time-consuming yet essential activities of data sensemaking is exploratory data analysis. Before we can answer specific questions with data, we must get the lay of the land. Exploring data in a free-form manner and examining it from every perspective creates a mental model that serves as the overview of the forest with a clear orientation to our surroundings that's needed before venturing in among the trees. Exploring data in this manner takes a great deal of time, but how many organizations allow us to build this into our schedules? Relatively few. This needs to change. Thinking critically and scientifically with data requires a firm investment in time.

Also, as I pointed out in "Chapter 6 – Develop Good Thinking Habits," we must manage our attention carefully to avoid distraction. This requires a distraction-free space. Our organizations must provide work environments that support deep and uninterrupted thinking. This includes rooms with doors and permission to disconnect from others for long periods of time. This can come with a cost, but it's worth it.

Invest in Data-Sensemaking Skills

For several years now the work of data sensemakers has been undermined by the myth of self-service analytics. Unlike pumping our own gas, data sensemaking is highly skilled work. As long as our organizations embrace the myth of self-service, the work of data sensemaking will be trivialized as something that anyone can do. Organizations that think critically and scientifically with data recognize self-service analytics for what it is: a marketing myth that serves no one but the vendors that promote it. Techno-magical solutions are enticing, but they aren't real. Critical and scientific thinking embrace the world as it is. The better world that we desire won't be wished into existence. It will be ushered in by hard-won skills.

As I mentioned in the first chapter, the only training that most data sensemakers have received is in the use of one or more analytical tools. This provides little instruction in the actual skills that are needed to make sense of data and gives a false sense of competence. In fact, training in a poorly designed analytical tool actually does great harm by encouraging ineffective data-sensemaking practices.

Training in data-sensemaking skills, especially those that we've examined in this book, doesn't fall into the *nice-to-have* category. These skills are essential, but our employers rarely give us an opportunity to pursue them. As a consequence, unless we acquired these skills in college, we're forced to pursue them on our own time. Those of us who care deeply about our work will do what it takes to become skilled, but we shouldn't have to work so hard. Smart organizations identify the skills that their people need and create opportunities to develop those skills. This requires funding. Employees must be allowed to set time aside for learning. These costs can sometimes be paid back by a single insight that comes when a skilled data sensemaker interacts with the organization's data. The greater our skills, the more often this will happen.

Cultures are difficult to change, and change doesn't happen overnight. There is no magical means to make this happen. We must persuade those who hold the reins in our organizations to embrace critical and scientific thinking. Using the strategies outlined in this book—building a loom of critical and scientific thinking with which to weave data into a fabric of understanding—we can model these thinking skills and demonstrate through our work that cultivating them is worth the price.

EPILOGUE – EMBRACE THE OPPORTUNITY

Data sensemakers are uniquely privileged. We have an opportunity to do important work. By helping people understand the world better, based on data, we can contribute to informed decisions and actions. Even though the expression "making the world a better place" has been trivialized through excessive, superficial, and often inauthentic use, it's still worth pursuing. It's what motivates me to sit at my desk and immerse myself in data. It's certainly what motivated me to write this book.

Decisions and actions that are based on critical and scientific thinking are almost always better than those that aren't. Rooted in understanding, they promote the survival and flourishing of our species. We need this desperately. If we fail to do this better than we have so far, our world will suffer. In a world that increasingly relies on data for understanding, we must learn to think in these ways.

While I was putting the finishing touches on this book, I watched a science documentary that affected me profoundly. The documentary followed several scientists from various domains as they engaged in their work, doing what they love. Their joy brought tears to my eyes. It was infectious. It gave me hope that we as a species aren't totally screwed. A lot of crap goes on in the world that leaves me discouraged and, at times, downright depressed, but the enthusiasm of these scientists was a soothing balm. As data sensemakers, we can approach our work with similar commitment and enthusiasm. If we took our work seriously enough and prepared for it as good scientists prepare for theirs, we could make important discoveries; we could greet each day with hope, eager to weave data into meaningful, true, and enlightening tapestries. Our work can make a difference, but only if we're prepared to do it well.

Thinking critically and scientifically with data is not enough to solve our problems. These skills form the foundation of data sensemaking, but they must be combined with other skills to get the job done, including statistical thinking, systems thinking, visual thinking, and ethical thinking. I believe that the final item on this list—ethical thinking—is especially important. Understanding alone doesn't guarantee good decisions and actions. It can also be used to do harm. In and of itself, understanding isn't the endgame. Once we've developed the loom that's needed to weave data into understanding, we must proceed from there to wisdom. We demonstrate wisdom when we put understanding to work in the form of decisions and actions that create the best possible outcomes.

I sincerely hope that you've found this book useful. It takes great effort and skill to do the work of data sensemaking well. At times, it even takes courage. And always, it's an act of love—or should be. Our world is precious; we dare not waste it. Humankind is a precious experiment; we dare not stagnate or regress.

I wish you well, for all our sakes.

Steve

REFERENCES

Chapter 1

1. Millay, Edna St. Vincent. 1939. "Huntsman, What Quarry?"
2. Noon, Randall K. 2009. *Scientific Method: Application in Failure Investigation and Forensic Science.* CRC Press. p. xviii.
3. Beveridge, W. I. B.. 1957. *The Art of Scientific Investigation.* New York, NY: W. W. Norton and Company, Inc. pp. 3-4.
4. Kida, Thomas. 2006. *Don't Believe Everything You Think.* Amherst, NY: Prometheus Books. p. 15.

Chapter 2

1. Dewey, John. 1909. *How We Think.* Boston, MA: D.C. Heath and Co.. p. 9.
2. Paul, Richard, Alec Fisher, and Gerald Nosich. 1993. "Workshop on Critical Thinking Strategies." Sonoma State University, Foundation for Critical Thinking. p. 4.
3. Paul, Richard and Linda Elder. 2001. *Critical Thinking: Tools for Taking Charge of Your Learning and Your Life.* Upper Saddle River, NJ: Financial Times Prentice Hall.
4. Kahneman, Daniel. 2011. *Thinking, Fast and Slow.* New York, NY: Farrar, Strauss and Giroux. p. 25.
5. Ibid. p. 36.
6. Ibid. p. 12.
7. Gauch, Hugh G., Jr. 2012. *Scientific Method in Brief.* Cambridge, UK: Cambridge University Press. p. 115.
8. Carroll, Sean. 2016. *The Big Picture.* New York, NY: Dutton. p. 41
9. Ibid. p. 71.
10. Ibid. p. 72.
11. Huxley, Leonard. 1901. *Life and Letters of Thomas Henry Huxley,* Vol. 1. New York, NY: D. Appleton and Company. p. 235.

12. Kahneman, Daniel. 2011. *Thinking, Fast and Slow.* New York, NY: Farrar, Strauss and Giroux. p. 114.

13. Gilovich, Thomas. 1991. *How We Know What Isn't So.* New York, NY: The Free Press. p. 9.

14. Gould, Stephen Jay. Quoted by Steve Dunn. May 31, 2002. "The Median Isn't the Message." *CancerGuide.* <https://www.cancerguide.org/median_not_msg.html>

15. Ibid.

16. Barr, Stacey. 2017. *Prove It!* Milton, Australia: John Wiley & Sons Australia. p. 93.

17. Pearl, Judea and Dana Mackenzie. 2018. *The Book of Why: The New Science of Cause and Effect.* New York, NY: Basic Books. pp. 5-6.

18. Ibid. p. 6.

19. Ibid. p. 21.

Chapter 3

1. American Association for the Advancement of Science. 1989. "Science for All Americans: A Project 2061 Report on Literacy Goals in Science, Mathematics, and Technology." p. 28.

2. Pirsig, Robert M. 1974. *Zen and the Art of Motorcycle Maintenance.* New York, NY: William Morrow & Co. pp. 100-101.

3. Ridley, Matt. 1999. *Genome: The Autobiography of a Species in 23 Chapters.* New York, NY: Harper Perennial. p. 271.

4. Carey, Stephen S. 2011. *A Beginner's Guide to Scientific Method,* Fourth Edition. Boston, MA: Wadsworth Cengage Learning. p. 58.

5. Noon, Randall K. 2009. *Scientific Method: Application in Failure Investigation and Forensic Science.* CRC Press. p. 27.

6. Carey, Stephen S. 2011. *A Beginner's Guide to Scientific Method,* Fourth Edition. Boston, MA: Wadsworth Cengage Learning. p. 30.

7. Gauch, Hugh G., Jr. 2012. *Scientific Method in Brief.* Cambridge, UK: Cambridge University Press. p. 26.

Chapter 4

1. Paul, Richard and Linda Elder. 2001. *Critical Thinking: Tools for Taking Charge of Your Learning and Your Life*. Upper Saddle River, NJ: Financial Times Prentice Hall. p. 113.
2. Carey, Stephen S. 2011. *A Beginner's Guide to Scientific Method, Fourth Edition*. Boston, MA: Wadsworth Cengage Learning. p. 10.
3. Niederman, Derrick and David Boyum. 2003. *What the Numbers Say*. New York, NY: Broadway Books. pp. 49-50.

Chapter 5

1. Muller, Jerry Z. 2018. *The Tyranny of Metrics*. Princeton, NJ: Princeton University Press. p. 4.
2. Kelvin, Lord William Thomson. 1883. "Electrical Units of Measurement." *Popular Lectures*, Vol. I. p. 73.
3. Cameron, William Bruce. 1963. *Informal Sociology: A Casual Introduction to Sociological Thinking*. New York, NY: Random House. p. 13.
4. Hubbard, Douglas W. 2007. *How to Measure Anything*. Hoboken, NJ: John Wiley & Sons. p. 33.
5. Gregg, Alan. 1941. *The Furtherance of Medical Research*. Oxford, UK: Oxford University Press. p. 8.
6. Barr, Stacey. 2017. *Prove It!* Milton, Australia: John Wiley & Sons Australia. p. 61.
7. Ibid. p. 62.
8. Niederman, Derrick and David Boyum. 2003. *What the Numbers Say*. New York, NY: Broadway Books. pp. 13-14.
9. Barr, Stacey. 2017. *Prove It!* Milton, Australia: John Wiley & Sons Australia. p. 71.
10. Ibid. p. 134.
11. Transocean Ltd. April 2, 2011. Quoted by Jeff McMahon. "Transocean Execs Get Bonuses after 'Best Year in Safety,' Despite Gulf Oil Disaster." *Forbes*. <https://www.forbes.com/sites/jeffmcmahon/2011/04/02/transocean-bonuses-deepwater-horizon-gulf-spill/#d86354d48790>

12. Muller, Jerry Z. 2018. *The Tyranny of Metrics*. Princeton, NJ: Princeton University Press. p. 180.

13. Niederman, Derrick and David Boyum. 2003. *What the Numbers Say*. New York, NY: Broadway Books. p. 233.

14. Muller, Jerry Z. 2018. The Tyranny of Metrics. Princeton, NJ: Princeton University Press. pp. 53-55.

15. Ibid. p. 121.

16. Ibid. p. 20.

17. Deming, W. Edwards. 1993. *The New Economics*. Cambridge, MA: MIT Press. p. 41.

Chapter 6

1. Newport, Cal. 2016. *Deep Work: Rules for Focused Success in a Distracted World*. New York, NY: Grand Central Publishing. p. 3.

2. Ibid. pp. 5-6.

3. Ibid. pp. 69-70.

4. Walker, Matthew. 2017. *Why We Sleep*. New York, NY: Scribner. p. 68.

5. Ibid. 296.

6. Ibid. 7.

7. Ibid. 53.

INDEX

A Beginner's Guide to Scientific Method 52, 54, 69, 126–127

Abduction (form of logic) 21–22

accuracy (of data) 75–76

"A Course of Study in Analytical Thinking" 6

aggregation (of data) 79–80

Allen, David 107

American Association for the Advancement of Science 49, 126

anchoring effect 26–27

appeal to accomplishment 28

appeal to authority 28

appeal to coincidence 28

appeal to common belief 28

appeal to common sense 28

appeal to consequences 28

appeal to desperation 28

appeal to emotion 28

appeal to intuition 29

appeal to nature 29

appeal to trust 29

arguments (vs. descriptions) 18–20, 22

Aristotle 19

attention 103–107

availability heuristic 24–25

Barr, Stacey 39, 85, 87, 92, 126–127

base rate 33–35

base rate fallacy 33–35

Bayes Theorem 21

Bayes, Thomas 21

Bayesian statistics 21–22

beliefs 13, 20–21, 23, 28, 49

Bennett, Bo 46

Beveridge, W.I.B. 4, 125

biased sample fallacy 31

Big Data 41, 44–45, 75, 78, 90

Boyum, David 74, 86, 91–92, 127–128

breadth (of thinking) 15

British Petroleum 88

business intelligence 10

Cameron, William Bruce 84, 127

Carey, Stephen S. 52, 54, 69, 126–127

Carroll, Sean 20–21, 125

categorical data 67–68

causal errors 40–46

Causal Revolution 40

causation 40–45, 63, 78

central tendency (measures of) 37–39, 71, 80, 91 94–95

cherry picking 31

cholera 42–43

clarity 14

clearing the mind 107

cognitive biases 16–18, 46

collaboration 65–66, 108

completeness (of data) 76

complexity 114

conclusions (of arguments) 13–15, 18–22

confirmation bias 22–24, 53

confounders (as in confounding variables) 61–62

context (of data) 77, 113

control chart (a.k.a., process control chart) 97

control group 51, 58, 61

controlled variables 52, 61

correlation 41–42, 44–45, 78

creativity 100, 106, 109–110

credences 21

critical thinking 13–15

Critical Thinking: Tools for Taking Charge of Your Learning and Your Life 14, 67, 125, 127

critique 116–117

data analysis 10

data science 10

data sensemaking 10–11

data storytelling 112

daydreaming 106–107

decision factories 111

deduction (form of logic) 18–20

deep work 104–105

Deep Work: Rules for Focused Success in a Distracted World 104–105, 128

Deepwater Horizon 88

default effect 25–26

default mode (of the brain) 106

Deming, W. Edwards 100–101, 128

dependent variable 51–53, 61

depth (of thinking) 15

description (vs. arguments) 18–19

descriptive statistics 92

Dewey, John 13, 125

directed data sensemaking 69

disconfirmation 53, 55, 62

distraction 103–107

documentation (of research) 63–65

domain knowledge 2–3

Don't Believe Everything You Think 8–9, 125

dreams 109–110

Dresner, Howard 10

Elder, Linda 14, 67, 125, 127

"Electrical Units of Measurement" 84, 127

empirical 48–49, 55

ethical thinking 3, 122

experiments 50–51, 57–59

explanations 20–21, 28, 47, 50, 54

exploratory data sensemaking (a.k.a., exploratory data analysis) 68–69

expression (of data) 81

falsifiability (of science) 49, 54–55

familiarity errors 22–30

faulty reasoning 15–16

Fisher, Alec 13, 125

Galileo 27

Gauch, Hugh G. 20, 55, 125–126

Genome: The Autobiography of a Species in 23 Chapters 50, 126

Getting Things Done 107

Gilovich, Thomas 35–36, 126

Gould, Stephen Jay 38–39, 126

Gregg, Alan 85, 127

habits (as in, thinking habits) 42, 103

halo effect 31

hasty generalization error 30

heuristics 17

histogram 94–95

homogeneity 31, 39, 93–94

hot-hand fallacy 35–36

How to Measure Anything 84, 92, 127

How We Know What Isn't So 35–36, 126

How We Think 13, 125

Hubbard, Douglas 84, 92, 127

"Huntsman, What Quarry?" 1, 125

Huxley, Leonard 23, 125

Huxley, Thomas 23, 125

hypotheses 24, 50, 53–54, 56–59, 62–63

independent variable 51–52, 61

induction (form of logic) 18–21

Informal Sociology: A Casual Introduction to Sociological Thinking 84, 127

Kahneman, Daniel 16–17, 30–31, 46, 111, 125–126

Kelvin, Lord William Thomson 84, 127

Kida, Thomas 8–9, 125

law of small numbers 30–31

law of the instrument 29–30

Levitin, Daniel J. 108

Life and Letters of Thomas Henry Huxley 23, 125

life sciences 48

logic 15, 18–19, 48

Logically Fallacious 46

logicalness 15

Luhn, Hans Peter 10

Mackenzie, Dana 40, 126

Mark, Gloria 103

Math with Bad Drawings 99

McKinsey 105

mean (statistical) 39, 71, 79–80, 94–95

measures 37–38, 83–101

median (statistical) 38–39, 80, 95

"Median Isn't the Message, The" 38–39, 126

memory 107, 109

mental models 20, 27

mere exposure effect 24

metacognition 18

Method of Agreement 41–42

Method of Concomitant
    Variation 42

Method of Difference 42

metrics 83–101

Mill, John Stuart 41–42

Millay, Edna St. Vincent 1,
    125

Mill's Methods 41–42

mindfulness meditation 131

mistakes 8, 117–118

monitoring (of data) 97–98

Muller, Jerry Z. 83–84, 90,
    98–100, 127–128

multiple regression analysis
    43

Naked Statistics 92

natural sciences 48

natural world 48

Newport, Cal 104–105, 128

Niederman, Derrick 74, 86,
    91–92, 127–128

Noon, Randall K. 2–3, 53–54
    125–126

normal distribution 72,
    94–95

Nosich, Gerald 13, 125

note-taking 107–108

Now You See It 92

NREM (non-rapid eye
    movement sleep)
    109–110

objectivity (of science) 55

observational studies 53–54,
    62

observations 18, 30–31,
    48–49, 69

Orlin, Ben 99

outcome bias 45–46

paradigms 27–28, 65

Paul, Richard 13–14, 67, 125,
    127

Pearl, Judea 40–41, 126

physical sciences 48

Pirsig, Robert 49, 126

population (statistical) 30–31,
    59–60

post hoc ergo propter hoc 43–44

precision 14

predictive statistics 92

premises (of arguments)
    18–19, 22

presuppositions 49, 55

problem-solving abilities
    109–110

proof surrogate (logical
    fallacy) 87

Prove It! 39, 85, 87, 92,
    126–127

proxies 87–89

quantitative data 67–68

randomness 35–36, 78, 114

rankings 96

regression fallacy 36–37

regression to the mean 37

relevance (of data) 15, 70–72

REM (rapid eye movement
    sleep) 109–110

replication (of experiments) 54

representative data 59–60

representative sample 60

research reports 64

Ridley, Matt 50, 126

risk-free zone 117–118

sample size 32–33

samples (statistical) 60

science 47–48

"Science for All Americans: A Project 2061 Report on Literacy Goals in Science, Mathematics, and Technology" 49, 126

scientific method 48–56

Scientific Method in Brief 20, 55, 125–126

Scientific Method: Application in Failure Investigation and Forensic Science 2–3, 53–54, 125–126

Scientific Revolution 49

scientific thinking 47

selective perception 23

self-correction (of science) 55

self-service analytics 5, 119

semantics (of data) 72–73

Semmelweis effect 27–28

Show Me the Numbers 92

Signal 37

significance 15

sleep 108–110

Snow, Dr. John 43

social sciences 48

soundness (of arguments) 19, 22

source (of data) 73–75

Spinoza, Baruch 35

spurious correlation 44–45

statistical errors 30–39

Statistical Process Control (SPC) 37, 97–98

statistical thinking 3, 30, 114

status quo bias 25

strength (of arguments) 20, 22

syllogism 19

System 1 and System 2 thinking 16–18

systems thinking (a.k.a., systems theory) 3, 77

tentativeness (of science) 55

The Art of Scientific Investigation 4, 125

The Big Picture 20–21, 125

The Book of Why: The New Science of Cause and Effect 40, 126

The Furtherance of Medical Research 85, 127

The New Economics 100–101, 128

The Organized Mind 108

The Tyranny of Metrics 83–84, 90, 98–100, 127–128

theories 54

Thinking, Fast and Slow 16–17, 30–31, 46, 111, 125–126

time (importance of) 118

Transocean 88, 127

transparency (of science) 54–55

uncertainty 113

Understanding Variation 37

unit bias 45

validity (logical) 19–20, 22

variables 51–53, 61–62, 68

variation blindness 37–39

visual thinking 3

Walker, Matthew 108–110, 128

What the Numbers Say 74, 86, 91–92, 127–128

what-if analysis 40

Wheelan, Charles 92

Wheeler, Donald 37

Why We Sleep 109–110, 128

"Workshop on Critical Thinking Strategies" 13, 125

Zen and the Art of Motorcycle Maintenance 49, 126